P9-DOD-687

"With her enchanting prose and transcendent vision, she is indeed a florist's daughter—a purveyor of beauty—as well as a careful, tablet-wielding investigator, ever contemplative, measured, and patient in her charge."
—*Publishers Weekly*, starred review

"With delicate precision and wry humor and in a style at once poetic and spare, [Hampl] recounts her years growing up in St. Paul, MN. This wistful air coloring her writing is well balanced by her fond yet dry characterization of the colorful, sometimes caustic mother of Hampl's younger years. A thoughtful and elegant memoir."—*Library Journal*

"[Hampl's] style moves easily from the high lyricism of wonder and delight to the unfooled coolness of irony and skepticism . . . [It's] as if she were attending closely to a text, pressing the juice out of every sentence and paragraph and translating it into her own luminous words."—*Minnesota Star Tribune*

"This is an utterly beautiful book. Hampl is a poet, and her prose is rich and dense with image and meaning."
—*Baltimore Sun*

"Hampl has written several memoirs but none better than this one."—*Arizona Republic*

"Patricia Hampl has written several memoirs, but none better than *The Florist's Daughter* . . . she re-creates them with honesty and intelligence, a tribute to them and to her skills as a writer."—*Detroit Free Press*

The Florist's Daughter

Also by Patricia Hampl

PROSE

Blue Arabesque

I Could Tell You Stories

Virgin Time

Spillville
(with engravings by Steven Sorman)

A Romantic Education

POETRY

Resort and Other Poems

Woman Before an Aquarium

AS EDITOR

The St. Paul Stories of F. Scott Fitzgerald

*Burning Bright: An Anthology of Sacred Poetry
from Judaism, Christianity and Islam*

The Florist's Daughter

PATRICIA HAMPL

Mariner Books   Houghton Mifflin Harcourt
Boston   New York

First Mariner Books edition 2009

www.hmhbooks.com

Library of Congress Cataloging-in-Publication Data
Hampl, Patricia,
The florist's daughter : a memoir / Patricia Hampl.—1st ed.
p. cm.
1. Hampl, Patricia—Childhood and youth. 2. Poets, American—
20th century—Biography. 3. Daughters—United States—Biography.
4. Saint Paul (Minn.)—Social life and customs. I. Title.
PS3558.A4575Z466 2007
818'.5403—dc22
[B] 2007004403
ISBN 978-0-15-101257-2
ISBN 978-0-15-603403-6 (pbk.)

Text set in Electra LH
Designed by Lydia D'moch

Printed in the United States of America

BTA 10 9 8 7 6 5 4 3 2

For my brother Peter

The Florist's Daughter

Chapter 1

FOR ONCE, NO FLOWERS. Past midnight and very quiet along this corridor. The clock on the opposite wall is round, a cartoon clock. Funny, the idea of *keeping time*—here of all places. Beneath the clock, a square calendar announces in bold what is now the wrong date, April 3.

I could walk over, just a few steps, tear the page away from the calendar, and make it today, April 4. But that would cause a ripping sound, and I'd have to let go of her hand. So, leave it. In this room it's yesterday. We won't reach today until this is over, the time warp we entered three days ago. She'd appreciate that, irony being her last grasp on reality.

"This time," the doctor said in the hallway last night—it might have been two nights ago—"you understand this time, this is it?"

Five years ago I had faced him wild-eyed in the ER after her first stroke. "What do you want us to do?" he had asked then.

What do *I* want you to do? I have a graduate degree in lyric poetry, what do I know? But I heard myself say, "Treat her like a sixteen-year-old who's just crashed on her boyfriend's motorcycle."

And he did. They did. The whole high-tech array of surgical, medical, therapeutic systems revved into high gear.

But this time I don't try to save her. I look at the doctor, by now my accomplice, and I say *Oh yes* when he says *You understand...this is it*, eager to prove myself no trouble, a maker of no fuss. Not something she could be accused of. "I get the feeling your mother doesn't...like me," he confided a year ago, this mild man of goodwill and even better bedside manner. "I walk in the room and she scowls. As if she *hates* me."

You got that right. I experience a surge of perverse pride at her capacity to alienate those with power over her, the self-immolating integrity of her fury. Her essential unfairness, throwing guilt like a girl, underhand. For her, no such thing as an innocent bystander. Cross her path and the poisoned dart springs from the quiver of her heart. *The look.* Narrowed eyes, pinched disdainful mouth, brilliant mime of venomous dislike. I know it well, doctor. "You Goody Two-shoes," she spit out once when I was cleaning her apartment, mopping up cigarette ash around her chair. She didn't bother to disguise her contempt for me as a nonsmoker—obviously, I didn't know how to enjoy life.

But that sour face of her elderly fury keeps disappearing just as she is disappearing. Even this latest face, the one propped on the hospital pillow, the hieratic visage that seems polished and will soon be an object, even this one is hard to keep in focus. I'm sitting here, holding her hand, but it's the ardent face from 1936 that keeps appearing, the face in the photograph placed on the shelf above the piano all the years of my girlhood and beyond. Heart-shaped with high cheekbones and eyes set wonderfully wide, it is the face of a romantic lead.

Not because she was beautiful—she wasn't beautiful. She was seriously pretty, the way Scott Fitzgerald described the real heartbreakers. The slightly dazzled eyes (she refused to wear her glasses) looked out with a shyness clearly feigned. That was the entrancing part—you could tell she wasn't really shy. She was happy. And a little startled by it. She couldn't keep the happiness of her body-and-soul off her face. Neither could my father—because of course he's standing next to her. Though not yet my father, not yet her husband.

Both of them gaze directly at the camera, standing by a cottonwood tree on a sandy bank of the Mississippi. Springtime from the look of the tree, site of a picnic, no doubt. She slouches her trim self stylishly, just touching his lean body. A claim being made. She's happy and he looks . . . proud. They both have a slightly abashed shyness stamped on their faces. Good-lookers. They're stepping into their future, he in an open-neck shirt, she in jodhpurs and a little leather jacket. It's their first picture together.

I stared at it all my girlhood as if at a problem to be solved—who *are* these people?—while I tooled my way through a Chopin mazurka, a Bach prelude, under the erotic glory of two kids crazy in love who looked down from another planet, not the one we inhabited together—Mother, Dad, Peter, me—in our bungalow on Linwood Avenue.

"The nurses can set up a cot for you," the doctor said last night. The low cot is wedged next to her now. I'm perched on the edge, barely hoisted above the floor, a supplicant crouched below the elevated royal bed. I gaze up at the tiny body, the porcelain face. There's a yellow legal pad on my lap. I'm a notetaker from long habit.

It's her habit, in fact, one I borrowed or inherited or stole from her. Note-taking, newspaper clipping, file making, all the librarian traits of wordiness and archival passion she displayed. Her favorite books were biographies (how smoothly the past tense inserts itself already), big thumpers of Dolley Madison and Abigail Adams on the American history side, Parnell and Wolfe Tone for the Irish obsession. And now on the yellow legal pad, the beginning of hers:

HAMPL, Mary Marum
Age 85
Mary Catherine Ann Teresa Eleanor Marum Hampl
born July 26, 1917, in St. Peter, MN, to Martha Smith

and Joseph Marum. The family moved to St. Paul when she was five, and she lived the rest of her life in this city she loved, in "God's country," as she always called Minnesota. A 1935 graduate of Mechanic Arts High School, she married her classmate Stanislaus Hampl in 1940 in the St. Paul Cathedral. They were together 58 years until Stan's death in 1998...

That's as far as I've gotten, having made the first artistic decision—loading on all the pretty names. They make her sound like a crowned head. I always wondered if she conferred most of them on herself.

I should probably put in her astrological sign. She was always glad to give it, raising her flyaway mane imperiously above her petite frame to say, "I'm Leo—the Lion." She liked to read my horoscope aloud (placid Pisces) in the morning after she read hers, and my father's and brother's (both the Bull, as men should be), to see how we were all doing, cosmically speaking. "Too bad," she would say sympathetically after giving me the wan future Jeane Dixon so often predicted for my watery self.

Not until the night nurse stops in and glances down does it occur to me that composing my mother's obit with my left hand as I hold her unconscious hand with my right might strike an outsider as offensive. Not to *her*, I want to protest. She would have expected nothing less, the dutiful writer-daughter scribbling in the half-light, holding the dying hand while hitting the high points of her subject's life that is finally going to see print. For a great reader, this is a great death.

SHE'S GLAD I'M HER DAUGHTER ("I'm proud of you," she says with some frequency), but for this I'm required to play my role, to be the Writer. "Are you working?" she asks, ever aware of any slacking off. Writing is my vocation—her word, the word of my upwardly mobile Catholic childhood. For years after she retired from her job at the library, she devoted herself to cataloging all my work, any scrap I had written. *I spent the day working on the Archive.* Yet she really thought being a librarian would have been the better choice: nicer to spend a lifetime reading than tied to a desk forever doing homework—because what else is writing?

Tonight I keep writing, the old habit. There's a lot to say about Mary Catherine Ann Teresa Eleanor. The roller ball moves smoothly across the blue lines, over the conveyer belt of the yellow legal pad. The night nurse pads in, and I look up briefly and smile.

But for once the nurse doesn't smile back, doesn't ask gently if she can get me something, coffee, a cookie. She touches the porcelain forehead, straightens the already smooth cotton blanket, walks out without a word, the frown hardened, the lips pursed.

A lifelong people-pleaser, I find I'm glad to be disapproved of. And who does this remind me of? *I don't give a damn,* she's often said these last, lost years. *I'm going down the drain, kid. Let's have a cig.*

I mention how she wrote to-the-barricades letters to the *St. Paul Pioneer Press* "Mailbag" (the dual erosions of progressive politics and correct English usage were her chief concerns for Minnesota civilization—and *not* unrelated in her view). I'm pleased, on rereading, with the reference to "God's country," her little riff about Minnesota. I note that she was devoted to the Rosary. But I won't mention that she was fiercely antiabortion. A little censorship to keep the liberal politics undiluted by her priest-pleasing orthodoxy. *I'm praying for you,* she would say, eyes narrowed witchily. A hex, a jinx. *If I'd been for abortion, where would you be? Ha-ha!*

Her hand gives back no pressure but it's pleasantly cool. My hand is bigger than hers now, but it—my hand, not myself—*remembers* her hand, how it felt to be enclosed in hers, walking down Wabasha, as she strode along, not looking down at me, head held high, Leo the Lion negotiating the crowded summer sidewalk downtown. There's even a photograph of this moment, taken by one of the roving photographers of the 1950s who snapped candid shots on the street and then ran after you to sell them for a dollar. Strange to think she bought such a thing, she who watched every penny.

We're in front of Birdie's where my Czech grandmother "marketed," though my mother wouldn't be caught dead shopping there. "Birdie's is *filthy*," she said. Maybe she's just said that as the photographer snapped the picture because her face has a severe, disapproving look. Or maybe I mistake her determined expression for disapproval as she rushes through the downtown crowd, me trailing behind her, clearly straining to keep up. But it's a remark I heard more than once—*Birdie's is filthy.* An oblique Irish swipe at the Czech side of the family. *A mixed marriage,* one of the Irish great-aunts said. *She was meant for an Irish boy, a college boy. Your father had quite the movie-star looks. She went for the looks, don'cha know.*

At Birdie's, shiny tumescent fish lay on crushed ice next to mounds of bruised pears. Heavy green flies lofted above the stand. A man in a soiled white apron waved a northern pike in the air to clear the flies before he slapped the fish on butcher paper and wrapped it, marking the price with the grease pencil he kept tucked behind his ear. I wanted to stop, poke the fish with an index finger as my Czech grandmother did. But the cool, utilitarian hand of my young mother was pulling me away. I was an appendage, dragging at the side of her swishing skirt. She was keeping me from all this dirt, this *filth.*

I was magnetized by the word *filth,* or maybe by her disgust, which was charged with relish when she uttered it. The smell of fish, jeweled flies fussing over warm offal, the crush of people, and the casual rot that real life can't rid itself of— that was the future I aspired to. This dirt was more than a covert emblem of sex. It was the insignia of escape, the promise of liberation from the enclosure of the cool, purposeful hand of my mother. *Don't call it dirt,* one of the old Austrian growers said when I was playing near the mound of potting soil at the greenhouse where my father worked. *This here is soil, it's earth, this here.*

Maybe from that greenhouse reverence I sensed that filth was the essence of the Great World I longed for. I was meant for New York. And places like New York—Paris, of course, and Prague where the other side of family had come from, Africa and Asia in general, and San Francisco because it had a Chinatown.

I knew instinctively a real city had to be a mess if it counted at all. St. Paul was out of the running. *Yours from this hell-hole of life & time,* Scott Fitzgerald, my first literary hero, signed a letter, when he was stranded at home in St. Paul, to Edmund Wilson who existed on high in blessed Greenwich Village. My true destination, too. Just give me my ticket out.

So how is it I never got away? Strange, that I, family hippie, one-time pot smoker, and strident feminist who refused for years to marry, living in laid-back communes or *in sin* (my mother's voice) with the draft resister (*dodger,* my brother, scowling) that my family never liked but was faultlessly polite to—that this person, me myself in middle age and for years now happily married (*thank God,* my mother crowing) to *a good guy* (my father laconically okaying my true love)—that I ended up being the caretaker of my frail, failing parents. I who for so long made every effort to be selfish, to be unfettered (no marriage, no children), to organize my energies around poetry and travel, who spoke with august certitude about "my work" before there even was any, I who meant to *get out of here.*

Maybe it was my mother's fey clairvoyance and oracular readings from the newspaper horoscope that conscripted me to eternal daughterdom: *A son is a son until he takes a wife. A daughter is a daughter all her life.* Remember the note of triumph when she recited that rhyme?

And my father had his own lasso of love, his soft brown eyes apologetically radiating decency like vast wealth he wished to settle on me though, like all wealth, it came freighted with responsibility: *A guy has to do the right thing, no matter what the other guy is doing.*

So here I am, still dragging at her side, still living in the same old St. Paul neighborhood. Never have had anything but a Minnesota driver's license, never have lived more than a long walk from my girlhood home. Still a daughter. But soon, in hours apparently, I'll be nobody's daughter.

For years now I've sat in doctors' offices, waiting for my father or my mother, as they are dealt with by their medical handlers. I read magazines I never would read otherwise, *Ladies' Home Journal, Family Circle.* I seem to zero in on the articles on "parenting" (a word my own parents never used). Relentlessly bland narratives, replete with common sense or its obverse, tedious reassurance. I read them with rapt attention, especially those on the rebellious adolescent child, I who have no children.

It is "natural," also "inevitable," I read again and again,

that the child must grow away from ("reject" is the preferred word) the parent. It's the backdrop of the deeply held post-modern faith, the religion of self-realization I've tried to practice all my adult life—you must abandon ship in order to... what? To exist, to be a "self."

Becoming a person is the point. Being a child—a daughter—that's an interim position, a stunted condition. I've sat in the cardiologist's waiting room, in the neurologist's waiting room, attentively reading therapeutic bromides, as if I might finally get the message. Somewhere along the line, it seems, I neglected to *break away*. I remained the Daughter. *Boy, I don't envy you,* my oral-surgeon brother says from his safe perch on the West Coast where he's lived for decades.

Still holding her hand now, I glance away from the figurine my mother has become. I turn to the big window that is black and gives me nothing but my own face. Then I turn to the walls, the cartoon clock, the square calendar—the full compass of these days in this shadowy room. I'm waiting for light to break. It'll be another long night. The last one, probably.

In the dark, if I stare hard enough, the city reconfigures out the window, a ghostly replica of itself, shapes cast against the darkness. I can make out the form of the History Center. Beyond the History Center, the Cathedral that, from a different angle, I see from my own house. I'm close to home here, always.

———

FROM THE TOP WINDOW of the narrow brownstone where I live in this town I've never managed to escape, the illuminated dome of the St. Paul Cathedral rests top-heavy on the city's dominant hill, an improbable Jules Verne spaceship poised to observe the earthlings. The theatrical lighting also comes to us courtesy of the St. Paul Archdiocese that has decided, either out of civic generosity or from sheer self-regard, to indulge in the expense of the display.

Either way, thank you, thank you very much.

That's where they started it all. It was an August wedding because my florist father preferred summer, the growing season. Mother, the darker soul, favored late September, falling leaves, the first killing frost.

Did she ever get her way? Not then, not during her sweetheart period, not till later when she mastered the fine art of being impossible.

They settled on the thirty-first, as close to September as you could get without actually giving over to it. An overcast day, she used to say, as if in retrospect this augured poorly.

The Cathedral was her family parish, the Irish lighting candles before the altar of the Virgin Mother. He had no parish. His father, the Czech immigrant, growled through his stutter, *Priests are c-c-rooks.* But the Irish grandfather was an usher at Sunday Mass, *a pillar of the church* as the Irish great-aunts said.

On the arm of her father, the pillar, on the last day of August 1940, my mother came down the yawning center aisle of the bombastic nave whose immensity made even a nice crowd of family and friends look skimpy. A hired photographer documented all this. Big eight-by-ten glossies in a leatherette album fastened in place by black tabs, pictures so primal they're glued in mind more powerfully than memory itself, as if the twentieth century gave everybody an extra kit bag of memories, your own flimsy, inexact ones, and the incontrovertible evidence of photo albums, image upon unsorted image documenting your life before you existed. *I knew you before you were born*, the shirttail Irish relatives would say when they met me.

She was dressed in a chalk-white gown, the skirt formed by rows of lace flounces, the bodice topped with a mandarin collar and sprouting gossamer cap sleeves. She held no bouquet. She preferred to carry a book, as if she already divined her years as a library file clerk that lay ahead. The white kid-leather prayer book trailed satin streamers punctuated by stephanotis blossoms that her florist bridegroom had ingeniously wired to the ribbons. The dress was a knockoff of the one Vivien Leigh wears in the opening scene of *Gone With the Wind*. It had been mass produced for the brides of 1940. She was one of many Scarlett O'Haras that year.

Later, the dress, folded in sky-blue tissue paper, lived in a large waxed cardboard box pushed to the back of a closet where, over the course of my girlhood, it grayed into a strange yellow like an old bruise. It wasn't just a dress but something hallowed and creepy—a relic, the bleached bone of a saint.

When I learned in school about the Shroud of Turin, the disintegrating gown sprang to mind, dreadful in the dark of the airless closet, lying in its waxed box the size of a child's casket.

THESE APPARENTLY ORDINARY people in our ordinary town, living faultlessly ordinary lives, and believing themselves to be ordinary, why do I persist in thinking—knowing—they weren't ordinary at all?

What's back there? *Back there*, I say, as if the past were a location, geographic rather than temporal, lost in the recesses of old St. Paul. And how did it become "old St. Paul," the way I habitually think of it now, as if in my lifetime the provincial Midwestern capital had lifted off the planet and become a figment of history, and from there had ceased to exist except as an invention of memory. And all the more potent for that, the way our lives become imaginary when we try most strenuously to make sense of them.

It was a world, old St. Paul. And now it's gone. But I still live in it.

Nostalgia, someone will say. A sneer accompanies the word, meaning that to be fascinated by what is gone and lost is to be easily seduced by sentiment. A shameful undertaking. But nostalgia shares the shame of the other good sins, the way lust is shameful or drink or gluttony or sloth. It doesn't belong to the desiccated sins of the soul—pride, envy. To the sweet sins of the body, add nostalgia. The sin of memory.

Nostalgia is really a kind of loyalty—also a sin when misapplied, as it so often is. But it's the engine, not the enemy, of history. It feeds on detail, the protein of accuracy. Or maybe nostalgia is a form of longing. It aches for history. In its cloudy wistfulness, nostalgia fuels the spark of significance. My place. My people.

Another old–St. Paul way of thinking: Mother talking about her *people*, meaning not the nation, but the clutch of family streaming back to illiterate Kilkenny, her Irish grandfather who wouldn't take up a gun during the Traverse des Sioux "Indian Uprising" (*I couldn't shoot. I played with those boys*), her mother one of "the seven beautiful Smith girls, tall as men," and their one lone brother, feebleminded, wandering the street with a small tin drum. And he the handsomest of them all. Pity, pity.

Or she would say *my folks*, that mild Midwestern descriptor. My people, my folks, Mother and Dad—M & D in the private patois of the fervent journals I've kept all these years as if I were doing research for a historical novel forever incomplete because the research keeps proliferating. Until now. Now the research is almost done.

All these scattered bits I've collected that wait patiently, perfectly willing to be ignored, this being St. Paul, this being my folks.

But there's no ignoring it all now. No more clinging to duty in the old world with its humid kitchens and gossipy neighborhoods, its impacted furies and proud silences. Time's up, the wages of daughterhood are almost over.

But I'm still stuck, gazing at their faces that peer back, mute and demanding, from the wedding album, from the piano where I only *seemed* to be practicing Chopin, gazing back at their mysterious faces that should have been the most familiar faces in the world to me.

Nothing is harder to grasp than a relentlessly modest life.

I'VE DONE THE RESEARCH. I've got the evidence. Pick any of the notebooks off the shelf—each one turning to dust as old books and old dresses do. Moments, episodes, frustrations, exquisitely rendered injustices, scalpel-sharp character studies that draw a bead of blood along the line of a paragraph— they're packed away in old journals, left in my own airless closet as if swathed in blue tissue paper.

This one from April 1981 will do. She and I are walking past the flower shop downtown. Maybe we were going to stop by to say hello to Dad. I can't remember that and didn't record it. We'd been to lunch at the River Room in Dayton's department store.

I'm already past thirty, but we've been going to the River Room since I was six when she advised, *Order the Russian salad, darling.* The Russian salad had two anchovies laid across it in a limp, salty X. *You should know what an anchovy is.* She too had an instinct for the Great World where anchovies might be encountered from time to time. In spite of indenturing me (...*a daughter's a daughter*...), she didn't expect I'd be stranded in this proud Catholic town of fish sticks and "Friday menus" posted at the Grand Avenue restaurants. Without Minneapolis, we read with humiliation, what would we be? A cold Omaha.

But by 1981 even St. Paul had entered the new world order of quiche and croissants. The Russian salad of the Joe McCarthy years was off the menu, taking with it the risky glamour of pinko food. The new Frenchy *cuisine* had no such illicit allure. St. Paul took to it overnight. Glass of wine, too, another nouvelle touch. "Take your mother to lunch," my father said about that time. "She gets lonely." Both of them were starting to "doctor," as Mother said, the beginning of their long endings.

Maybe it was the glass of wine she'd had. Well, two. Maybe her new frailty. Suddenly she was on the sidewalk, had fallen somehow. Just collapsed. She howled in pain, clasped her arm. It was broken. Many bones would break before the end.

In my notebook I reported to myself: *Then she started sobbing, "I wish I were dead, I wish I were dead" right there on the sidewalk. People walked around us. Later, when he came to St. Joe's Hospital where I took her, D looked down and rubbed his bruised knuckle. He hurt it when he'd moved a wedding palm at the greenhouse. I wanted to sob—that he rubbed his knuckle. For her I felt—what did I feel? Nothing, just nothing. That can't be right, to feel nothing when she's crying she wants to die. No, I did feel something, I thought: she's lying, she doesn't want to die. A cold feeling, as if she ought to mean it.*

An ordinary middle-class Midwestern family, in other words. A cozy setting for heartlessness.

Such people, modest to a fault, assume they're unremarkable even in their passion, even as they go down in licks of flame. They think they're leaving themselves to silence and forgetting. That's okay, they don't mind. Isn't that what death is, anyway? And isn't that what an ordinary, decent life is?

They expect to be forgotten.

But they aren't forgotten. They're less gone now than they were in their prime. Now that he's gone and she barely lingers, they're everywhere, bits of mica glinting off the Cathedral granite.

From time to time someone asks where I live. "In the shadow of the Cathedral," I say automatically, as if to say "near the Cathedral" wouldn't give the exact location. In the shadow of the Cathedral, the shadow of their long lives.

Six bells, tall as persons, are housed in the massive belfry. They bang out the quarter hour. On the hour they make a bigger commotion. Living a block away, it's impossible to forget the Cathedral. It's always remarking on itself.

Inside people light candles, mostly by the Blessed Mother's altar. Weekday afternoons, an organ student sometimes gets permission to practice in the choir loft. You can feel the bass notes in your body. Much Bach, some Buxtehude, dogged repetition of difficult phrasing, the complications of a fugue abandoned, a folding chair scraping the stone floor.

Occasionally someone will set up an easel, trying to get

on canvas the rose window or the complex perspective of the place. I've seen people settled into the pews as if on a davenport at home, reading novels—Judith Krantz, Elmore Leonard. Here and there, scattered figures kneel, fingers skimming their beads. A few homeless people catnap in prudently chosen side pews.

But in these off-hours most people just stroll through, heads thrown back to take in the astonishing vault of the dome. It's riveted at the compass points with the four principal virtues, spelled out in massive gilt letters as if they held up the entire enterprise: FORTITUDE, TOLERANCE, PRUDENCE, JUSTICE. Midwestern virtues, especially the first three. The fourth is what we like to believe we're capable of. The real believers, like my father, think Justice is what life is poised upon, the impenetrable primer coat on existence that protects life from the rust and decay of uncaring, from cynicism and greed.

A bronze commemorative plaque is affixed to a pew just below the raised pulpit. In this pew, it reads, sat John F. Kennedy, President of the United States of America, when he attended the eleven o'clock Mass, October 7, 1962. Some of the front center pews still carry small metal nameplates. These are even older, left over from the age of pew rental, my Irish grandfather's era, the pillar who wore in his buttonhole a white carnation that gave off the sharp scent of clove, as he moved up the aisle with the red velvet–lined collection plate on its long wooden handle.

"Of course we couldn't give *that* kind of money," my mother said. "We never had a nameplate." Always eager to assure me of our modesty, our middling safety in the middle of the continent in the middle of the century. "You were born after the war, you're a peace baby," she would say, securing my well-being not only in life but in history. She even wanted me to understand that, according to my third-grade teacher, I was neither brilliant nor stupid. "You're in the middle," she said with obvious relief. The best place to be: the middle. No harm done there. That's us: smart enough, middle-class, Midwestern, midcentury—middle everything. Safe, safe.

The preferred pews of the upper classes belong to nobody now. Except to memory—if tarnished metal bearing a name that no longer brings anyone to mind is memory.

Both of them bequeathed their modesty—they thought—to the adored child. Yet they made sure to educate me out of silence, past the sweet safe middle they clung to and urged upon me. Reach for the stars, sweetie—and stay, stay right here.

I'd long been acquainted with the alien anchovy and I was already jaded when she was hurrying to introduce me to the croissant during its debut at the River Room.

It was the beginning of trying to get the story straight, the day she admitted she wished she were dead, the day she revealed to me my cold heart.

Chapter 2

SHE LINED US UP after dinner in the living room by the Magnavox to pray the family Rosary, but Leo the Lion was no simple believer. Her credo was a litany of tart judgments delivered from the observer's margin. In a way that was decisive for me, she modeled what it meant to be a writer without actually writing anything. But wait a sec (as she would say)—don't forget those letters to the *St. Paul Pioneer Press* "Mailbag."

She possessed natural distance, an acute eye, the willingness to size things up. She could stir the soup of detail to a narrative froth. There was even a touch of Irish magical realism: *Never speak ill of the little people*, she would say severely, *my grandmother spoke with them often.* Fairies, mild instances of clairvoyance, a flair for coincidence that Dickens would have blushed to employ—she claimed them all.

The Czech aunts, my father's older sisters, regarded her with mistrust, her nose always in a book, a look of exquisite boredom she didn't disguise as they swapped recipes for sweet rolls. *Food*, she said with withering scorn as the aunts launched into plans for dinner while they were serving lunch. I was pulled in both directions, drawn irresistibly to the rising sweet dough of the Czech side where good times were to be had, then back to the arch misgivings of my Irish mother and the abstract world of words she dished out.

My father's floral work cracked open a door to glamour, to sparkle and wonder. At the breakfast table at home, mornings after one of the big holiday parties he decorated at the St. Paul Hotel or the James J. Hill mansion, she and I would sit almost till noon as she reconstructed the previous evening, an operative being debriefed by her handler.

His association with St. Paul society ladies who spent their days planning dinner parties and charity balls gave us a peephole into the indulgences of the rich. "The rich" belonged to a world beyond us, yet my father consorted with them, knew their ways, was easy in their company. It was the age before $10 buckets of roses in the grocery store, before people casually tossed a cellophane bundle of $4 daisies in their shopping carts. Flowers belonged to the world of death and delight—funerals and weddings and holidays. Only the grandees of our town ordered flowers as an everyday thing.

May I help you was what you said to a customer. My father helped people. People whose flower bills mounted marvelously into the hundreds every month. We spoke with wonder of the rare $10,000 wedding, meaning the flowers came to that. This was a marriage to take seriously.

I sat with my elbows on the kitchen table, face cupped in my hands as my mother talked. She had a superb reading voice, free of melodrama, embodying the *sangfroid* of a story's ups and downs, conveying the remorseless inevitability of fiction. Her speaking voice, as she told her own stories, had this same reportorial authority. The dry voice looped on, constructing the party scene meticulously until the previous night was propped before us on our chipped red-and-white enamel kitchen table, a maquette made of nothing but words.

"You know what Shakespeare called words?" she said, still gleaning happily from the stubble fields of her high-school English classes (there had been no college for either of them). *"Airy nothings!"*

But what Shakespeare really meant, what she believed too, was that words were everything. They could go anywhere, be anything. They got you to the Great World without a ticket. I told her, sometime after she read me *Charlotte's Web*, not stopping as I keened, reading through my heartbreak over the tragic ending, that I was going to be a writer. *Yes*, she said thoughtfully in response to this, *you've got the gift of gab.*

Trusting no one, she saw literature not simply as art but as a way of getting the last word, a subset of self-righteousness, a consolation prize for the defeated. And therefore a worthy use of a person's energies. For my father, who trusted everyone and saw art in the service of beauty, literature was not the higher court she took it to be. He saw language as a form of manners, an aspect of behavior. And manners, it went without saying, were an art form too, the art of daily life. When, late in life, an eye surgeon bungled my mother's cataract surgery, leaving her blind in one eye and the other failing, my father wanted to pay the bill—out of regard for the man's feelings. "We all make mistakes, Mary," he said.

She tore up the bill and sent the pieces back in an envelope with a rich letter worthy of the *Pioneer Press* "Mailbag." Some years later we heard the doctor had lost his license and was selling real estate. Neither of my parents would ever have considered a lawsuit.

"You two still sitting there?" my father would say incredulously, passing by the kitchen table on the way to some project he had going in his workroom in the basement. A man of many projects and few airy nothings.

SHE WAS EVEN THE CARETAKER of stories from the Czech side, including the one it seems I always knew, the one so embedded it wasn't really a story but a string of genetic code. It had a scary beginning, but it too veered off into our middling safety. A nothing-happened narrative, our kind of story.

Aunt Lillian, one of my father's older sisters, had been attacked one night. Right at the side of their house near West

Seventh. Attacked and *almost* raped. *Almost,* but saved in the nick of time. No harm done. My grandmother, the Czech peasant, came charging out of the house and stopped it before *the worst* could happen.

Lillian, ninety-five pounds and pretty, a dresser who finished high school because her twin brother, Frankie (who had dropped out to try his luck as a boxer), told her he'd buy her a diamond ring if she stayed on and graduated. *I lost that ring,* she would always say fretfully. That was her story, the loss of a ring, not how she *almost* was raped. That she never mentioned.

Mother told that one. Lillian had been to a dance downtown and came home on the streetcar, walking along the little cement divide between their house and the Korlats', the dark passageway to the back door (I knew it well). Someone jumped out from the dark and gagged her. Chloroformed her.

What's that?

Drugged her. A soaked rag over her face. It knocks you out.

What happened?

Nana saved her.

What happened to . . . him?

Oh, nothing. He was the son of a neighbor. They hushed it up. Lillian didn't remember anything.

Not now?

Nothing.

My stay-at-home aunt, ever in a domestic dither, checking the burners on her stove a dozen times a day to be sure all the knobs were turned to OFF, her ranks of Tupperware containers stacked in a kitchen cabinet, silver sheathed in Saran Wrap, her shoes housed in marked shoe boxes like relics in their reliquaries in the closet she reorganized in ever more meticulous order, this careful woman who rarely left her house and spent the entire day fixing dinner for her husband—she had escaped assault, she had only *almost* been raped. She remembered nothing. She had a husband who was crazy about her, Bill. They had no children and sang to each other and were happy—*Button up your overcoat... You belong to me!*

There was no story, just the lucky absence of a story. She'd been saved from *the worst*.

I DIDN'T LIKE MOTHER to start her party stories with people, with *action*, anyway. She used to try that, telling little vignettes, passing along a dry barb of gossip, building in background and subplots. Left to her own devices, she had an unfortunate tendency toward the cautionary tale. The story of the St. Paul lawyer ("a good customer of your dad's") and his young secretary found in the backseat of his Pontiac in a Highland Park cul-de-sac, motor running, the car's tailpipe jammed against a snowbank: dead in each other's arms, asphyxiated by backed-up carbon monoxide. Adultery with a Minnesota twist.

Or the little revenge tale she was determined to convey about the hot number she referred to as the Barefoot Contessa, a spoiled Summit Avenue girl who, years before and newly married, had tried to get my father to stay for drinks ("and who knows what else") when he was called in to discuss the possibility of root rot in her ficus tree. That one! Drunk as a lord last night and not the pretty thing she had once played at being.

Fat?

"I wouldn't say fat," she said judiciously, "but definitely… thickening."

Or the mother of three, wife of another florist, who ran off with her daughter's skating instructor—to California of all places ("not many rinks for them out there—ha!"). And the woman on Edgecumbe who always ordered flowers for her parents' graves in May—can you believe it, she swallowed a bottle of pills. That was the end of her. Apparently here too there was a backstory where heartbreak lurked, a secret lover, great sadness under cover of beautiful manners.

She developed a keen eye for reading a scene from the gestures of minor characters. Item: the woman at the St. Paul Hotel bar, head lolling while the husband said harshly, "You've had enough." The barman, she said, turning a detail worthy of Chekhov, looked away, practically strangled the rinsed shot glass in his hand with a bar towel.

But I discouraged this pursuit of character and plot development. *You have to start at the beginning.*

"What's the beginning?" she asked. I see now she was amused.

The beginning's where you tell what the room looked like.

Then you can let the people in. After. I wasn't after stories. I wanted the stage set of life. Location, location, location. I kept her to the surface, taking snapshots of my father's decorative world.

Weather and landscape were fine too. Our savage Minnesota winters were often the harrowing *mise-en-scène* lending necessary drama to our otherwise humdrum lives. Overlaying the impressively ruinous weather was the provincial touchiness of St. Paul's hierarchical social order whose weddings and parties, funerals and "affairs" my father planned and decorated. Something of setting, of our city and its stiff ways, insisted that truth was not folded away like lavender sachet with the dry goods of mere "character" or even in alarming action (the Pontiac in the snowbank, the Edgecumbe Road matron opening her bottle of pills).

The truth of existence was webbed into the organic structure of the atmosphere, in the eternal look and feel of things around us. We were part of that, residents of the provincial capital of God's country that Leo the Lion bound over in her photographic sentences as we sat at the kitchen table where everything was safe.

STICK WITH DESCRIPTION.

What was the room like? Describe the room, Ma.

Maybe I didn't long for the Great World after all, where risky things happened or almost happened. I craved my father's art, her sharp sketch of his craft working its charm on everyone. People were extras, called in by Central Casting to participate in my handsome father's magic. It hardly mattered what fool things they did in real life, what trouble they got themselves into. They were just assembled for the fete he created, brought in like so many Kentia palms rolled in as backdrops for touring theatrical productions that came to town from New York, or like lemon-leaf garlands pegged to a Summit Avenue mantelpiece in his artful holiday constructions.

My narrative restrictions seemed to liberate her. Once she understood her audience, she hit her stride. She described a serrated lemon slice floating in a finger bowl (no, you don't *eat* it!) and the mink stole that fell to the floor behind Mrs. Briarson's chair. "Oh, just leave it," said she. Imagine, not caring!

She was a master of the vignette.

I could count on a tally of the jewelry and a full shoe report—*Did anyone wear a pair of those clear plastic high heels that look like glass slippers?*

Several. A tone suggesting plastic shoes meant to imitate glass slippers were a mistake though she usually swept the debris of detail into her capacious descriptive holdall without resorting to approval or critique.

She could describe a vestibule for ten minutes, a veritable Proust of the breakfast table where we sat, she with her black coffee and pack of Herbert Tareytons, piercing the cellophane with a pointy red nail, pulling the thin blue band that bound it, tapping the enamel table until she nipped out a white cylinder. Her silver Ronson was in the shape of Aladdin's lamp. She snapped the flint and bowed her face like an acolyte to the flame. The oily scent of lighter fluid flushed the air. The sweet burn of tobacco clouded around us.

I sat before a congealed fried egg I would never eat no matter what she said about the starving children in China. It didn't matter. Her attention strayed to the black-and-white diamond-shape marble tiles that carried you past the glass double doors into the first parlor. New arrivals stamped their feet on the Persian carpet by the cloakroom. The fresh snow sparkled for a moment before it darkened to dampness. (People should always be encouraged to tramp fresh snow into a house—helps fight the low humidity of central heating, she said. A rare, but characteristically subversive, household hint.)

The panes of the glass doors were beveled. The light from the chandelier made little rainbows. *Rainbows*, I said, seeing them. She took a long drag, her hand on Aladdin's lamp. She knew how to let things sink in and shine and become real. She gazed off to the middle distance, not noticing me, going, going, gone.

But this was alarming. Was she still *here*? Or could this be a *sign*, the trigger of her...*condition*? She didn't permit us to use the word *fit*. She hated *seizure*. And *epilepsy* was absolutely forbidden. She reeled back to the nineteenth century for the word she could allow—*One of my spells*, she said.

A spell started that way, her face gazing off and up intently. An enthralled look indistinguishable from her story-telling face—celestial blue eyes fixed, lips in an abstracted smile as if she were seeing something miraculous in her mind's eye and might—or might not—tell you what it was.

But then a brutal fixity clamped the face, an awful rigidity robotized her body, things dropped from her taut hands. Convulsive jerking shook her, the mouth not smiling anymore, the jaw grinding. I was eleven the first time, Sunday morning after Mass, a terrible thud in the kitchen, pancake batter sloshed all over the stove, the stainless steel bowl still rolling across the floor when I got there. I was the first to reach her.

Grand mal, the doctor told us. The first French words I learned. Big bad.

But we didn't say *grand mal,* we didn't say *seizures.* As the years went by, punctuated now and again—not often—by these spectacular mime shows, she would sometimes refer to her condition more distantly as "what happens." Seizures were just *what happened.*

I understood she was made of volatile matter. Certain things—what were they?—could *set her off.* Later, when the Czech grandmother came to live with us, it was a terrible blow to my mother's independence, the presence of that Birdie otherness come into the house. One summer evening Nana came bustling onto the porch and Mother smiled gorgeously into the old peasant's face. I was so glad to see the usual look of impatience gone, replaced by that welcome. But then, in a mad twinkling, it was gone, *she* was gone, shuddering into *grand mal.* It was impossible to think she wasn't making a statement.

The rest of her life she took her medicine, two pills—one little, one big—three times, then later twice a day. Phenobarbital and Dilantin. The names were reassuring. Modern medicine had solutions. *Everything's under control,* my father said, his face taking on its own rigid set. *Your mother's fine.*

I once asked her if there was any advance notice, any indication it might...happen. She looked at me for a moment, hesitating (I had trespassed on forbidden territory). Then in a slow, shamed voice, "There's a ticking." Her index finger went to her temple, as if touching a locked canister. But from the outside where I watched, the signal was the beatific smile, her enthralled storytelling face.

She looked down, tapped her Tareyton lightly on the side of her plate as she described the night before. So everything was all right. For now. She hadn't been *set off.* Most of the time, as my father said, she was fine. Most of the time. But that was the thing: you never knew when the dreamy gaze might blossom into calamity. This gave her storytelling a heart-stopping note of suspense and danger.

A column of ash fell from her cigarette harmlessly, and she kept going, unfurling the airy nothings of the night before. This would have been one of her descriptions of the Summit Avenue mansion that had come into the possession of the Archdiocese sometime in the 1950s, and was used for charity balls. My father had done the flowers—that's why they were invited. *We aren't donors,* she explained unnecessarily. The people at the party were philanthropists, she said. *Rich?*

Certainly, she said. *Some can be very nice.*

She and my father were New Deal Democrats, Humphrey Democrats. Later, when I marched in protest against Humphrey during the Vietnam War, she was dismayed. *How can you be against Hubert?* He'd brought the Democrats and the Farmer-Labor Party together, she said, ever a Minnesota DFL champion.

He co-opted the Farmer-Labor Party, I replied from the certainties of my new poli-sci textbook lingo.

You don't remember 1948.

One of her points: Humphrey had been for civil rights before any of them. For her, he wasn't the apologist for the Johnson Administration—he was the northern idealist who'd stood up to the Dixiecrats.

She loved to tell the story of her high-school civics teacher who always voted for Norman Thomas. Had the woman thrown her vote away? Not at all! She'd voted her principles. That's what mattered, not winning, not losing. In fact, maybe losing was *better.* Losing was honorable, proved you had principles. Winning was power. And power proved nothing but itself.

But her real allegiance was to some anarchic guild of Irish grudge-bearers. Her eye for detail was lyric, but her vision burned with the acid of her potato-eating ancestors.

"They wouldn't let us learn to *read!*" she would cry full throttle, as if she had fought her way out of illiteracy beneath a hedgerow, "the English" stalking her contraband first-grade primer at Cathedral Elementary where the Sisters of St. Joseph, *thank God,* ran a tight ship.

And by the way, no Jesuits here. Archbishop Ireland wouldn't let them get a toehold in St. Paul, she said, glad to claim in the immigrant priest who built the Cathedral another mistrustful Irish heart.

Just look at the map—Jesuit colleges in Chicago, Milwaukee, Omaha, all the way west to Seattle. The missing link? St. Paul! (Minneapolis wasn't on her map, being Scandinavian and Lutheran, and therefore without spiritual substance.) You live in a Jesuit-free state. You can thank Archbishop Ireland for that. Never forget—the Jesuits ran the Inquisition.

And though you didn't want it in your own backyard, the Inquisition did not cast an entirely sinister shadow on Mother Church. Not for her, natural liberal though she was. The Inquisition conferred a dark majesty on the history she was part of, on history itself. It made her complicit with grandeur and danger, not a wan cipher lost in the flyover snowfields. We, right here, were part of the Church Universal, an essential bit of the DNA of the Mystical Body.

The world is eternally embattled, good and evil contend, people burn. That's history. You're part of that. Your father plants gardens in the summer and decorates parties in the winter. But life's no party, no matter how much we count on them, live off them. Life's a fight.

THE CHARITY BALLS she described were held in November or early December, before the holidays, before everyone (she said *everyone* though we both understood who this meant— not us) went to Florida. Some will go to Arizona, she said. Even Hawaii. Mrs. Bertrand to France. A villa near Nice. Imagine.

I imagined.

Go back, back to the room, I said if she started to follow the trail of one person or another. Describe the parquet floors, the shape of the crystal (yes, there was champagne, the glasses are called flutes, I don't know *why*), the buffet table (the shrimp lay in *mounds*, there was *lobster*).

She always gave a rhapsodic evocation of my father's table arrangements and his cunning ballroom decorations, and what people said about them. Much oohing and aahing, she reported. Oh *Stan!* the ladies said. We knew his matinee-idol looks were part of it. We could smile at the sighing charity ladies: after all, he was ours. That we never doubted. Only the flowers themselves might have a stronger claim on him, the petals panting in the moist glass houses on Banfil Street below the hill. The harem of fragile dependents my handsome father tended, even rising from bed in the middle of the night if the boiler went out in the winter.

Wealth impressed him, but also dismayed him. "It's the

cotillion crowd," he said once, "that don't pay their accounts or pay slow." Said with sad wonder, without rancor, as of a mysterious health problem in a good friend—diabetes or heart disease, something hereditary. An unfortunate condition beyond individual control. More to imagine—imagine not paying your bills, living beyond your means, imagine not having a budget. But they were gentlemen—a category he believed in, a caste he judged not by credit ratings but by manners.

"Your father trusts those *gentlemen* too much," she said, emphasizing the word with the same scorn she heaped on *the English*. Unlike him, she was ready to see an oppressor on the doorstep, a casual cheat in the accounting department, a hypocrite lurking behind a creamy smile.

I was on my father's side—the side of trusting people and pleasing them, the side of flowers and winking party lights. He and I had no argument with the apocryphal Fitzgerald remark that "the rich are different from you and me." Of course they are! They're supposed to be!

But she was likely to be right—I sensed that. Or perhaps I understood she had the world in sharper focus than he did. I resented her for it, as if she perversely turned on harsh fluorescent lights in a room gently glowing from beeswax candles he had placed there for the pleasure of all and the betterment of the world in general.

Leo the Lion only pretended to be a mouse in the corner. In fact, she could at any moment be *set off*, could explode. Somehow her irony and watchfulness and her seizures were balled up in my mind as part of the same thing. Put together, they were what made her sit at the kitchen table, talking, talking, describing the night before. I understood obscurely that she was on to something about life with all this describing. She owned it all with her talk, by turns sardonic and lyric, as my silent father earnestly plying his magic box of color and light did not.

She handled the money in the family (my father's idea), "reconciling" their checkbook to the penny (*and I mean penny*, she would say) every month at the dining-room table. She ticked off the canceled checks, bearing down so heavily that the X was embossed onto the next page, a ghostly tattoo of rectitude. The bundle of paid bills in their stamped envelopes sat with a red rubber band on the dining-room table for my father to put in the mailbox. *No account ever in arrears*, she would say with a satisfaction that was almost malicious, as if no one was going to catch *her*. Not the English, not the gentlemen, not the Jesuits, not First Grand Avenue Bank.

It was understood that my father couldn't keep track of household money to save his soul, a sure sign of an artistic nature. He had better things to think about—the big orders he supervised, the crops in the glass houses of the greenhouse. And though she too worked, first at an insurance company ("I love bookkeeping!") and later and most happily at a college library ("I love books!"), it was understood that these were just jobs, and lacked the demands of art that my father contended with.

Yet she was the one who *took things in*. Maybe art was not, after all, the making of beautiful things as my father was devoted to doing. Something unlovely and unblinking, unfooled and purposefully marginal was at the heart of it. A cool-eyed notetaker in the corner, getting it right, getting the last word, though unnoticed and mistaken for handsome Stan's birdlike wife.

We might live in St. Paul, pallid capital of the frozen flatland, but a significance of the sort I later recognized when I read the party scenes in Tolstoy radiated from the rooms my father decorated and my mother described. She could haunt an empty room with description as if readying it for trouble. End of a charity ball and she passes by the woody old Gopher Grille at the St. Paul Hotel on the way to the garage under the Lowry Medical Arts building where my father had parked the car.

The Grille is almost empty. Some of the heavy drinkers are still at it, murmuring at a dark table, having abandoned the ballroom when the private bar closed and the dancing began. They sit, the drinkers, beneath the rows of photographs of former Queens of the Snow from bygone St. Paul Winter Carnivals. *So sad*, Mother said, topping off her tableau with an enigmatic editorial caption.

What was sad? The drinkers huddled in the dark corner? The history of our civic beauties lost and faded? What? What? *So sad*, she said, shaking her head at the kitchen table, tapping her cig against her plate, like a good writer, refusing to explain what she had laid out for all to see.

She let the scene shimmer. Trouble twirled down the blue-and-gold wallpaper, infidelity winked in the gleam of the wood, embezzlement and sneaky deals were worn into the satin marble of the dead millionaire's house. *Can't you just see it?* she would say, taking another drag, exhaling while I made it all up in my mind's eye as she instructed, an intricate weave of delight and dirt, but one eye watching covertly to see if she was still with me, still in her right mind as she gazed off in that absent way of her storytelling, which was also the signal of one of her mysterious *spells*.

BUT I'VE MISSED THE POINT of my demanding description from her—no stories, no "characters," no "action." It was I myself who walked—floated—into these rooms my father designed, the rooms he made as complete and wonderfully intimate as the rooms in fiction. If I allowed her to fill in the space with other people's stories, where would I be?

There could be no better life than to take notes on the world as it passed by in all its oddity. This was my mother's way. It was poetry. But her astringent tone and sharp judgments cut into the loveliness of my father's no-fault world, the world that was made-up, that was art. The two of them only appeared to be united, kneeling in front of the Magnavox, toiling through the Holy Mysteries of the Rosary.

In fact, she wasn't his cheerleader, the innocent chronicler of his handiwork. She was a spy in the house of beauty, an ironist regarding the world he decorated so earnestly for people he trusted, people she regarded with a narrowed eye, waiting and seeing. *Up to no good*—the baleful phrase she employed so often I can't remember anyone specific it was meant for, though certainly for the owners of the floral business, her arch enemies, the prime takers-of-advantage of the too-trustful Stan, their faithful retainer. The ones she foreshadowed all my girl-hood as the cheats they proved, in time, to be.

I didn't want the deathly Pontiac rammed into the snow-drift, love and betrayal frozen in the backseat, or the aging Barefoot Contessa given her comeuppance. Description only, please, the spongy thinginess of life, the harmlessness my father purveyed, relayed across the kitchen table by my detail-sniffing mother. The heavy-jowled Victorian furniture of the Crocus Hill houses and the iced snowdrifts along the streets gave St. Paul a curiously historical look, bathing God's country in glittering significance, draped in the same white stasis year after year. Just give me that. It's enough.

She had even conscripted our own furniture for historical narrative purposes. During their yearlong engagement, some-time between leaning into each other under the cottonwood on the riverbank and the Scarlett O'Hara wedding day, they had bought the exquisitely uncomfortable pieces of Victorian dark wood and upholstery that we lived with our entire fam-ily life. The love seat, scrolled armrests set high, discouraged any form of affection. It looked like a purposely unforgiving settee used to keep hapless petitioners waiting, ramrod straight, before entering a chamber of power. She called it—and therefore we all called it—Napoleon. *It's French* was her only explanation. *Bring your aunt her old-fashioned. She's sitting on Napoleon.*

And the hideous, low-squatting little chair with the lion-faced armrests? That was Benito. *It's Italian.*

Two little dictators, gloomily commanding the living room. Mr. Williams was also there, the red mohair chair named for the kindly man who had sold them Napoleon and Benito. *He liked us, he knew we were setting up housekeeping.* Mr. Williams was a widower, he was breaking up his own house. A very sweet man, but of course heartbroken. This we knew, had always known, though we never met Mr. Williams. His story was part of the chairs, part of our story. A figment of their romance. I'm not sure when it dawned on me that other people didn't name their furniture.

Everything could be named, and, in naming, the world became permanent, eternal really. Because nothing changes here, nothing dies. Except flowers—that's the point of them. My father of course considered artificial flowers an affront, though in time he had to stock them. People buy flowers *because* they die, he said. To toss money at fleeting beauty—this was the point of buying flowers. Not their beauty, but their transience.

So let everything remain a stage set. Let me enter my father's lovely design, my father who believed the world was beautiful and made for more beauty, the creamy surface laid upon Justice that held up the world. Beauty was his job, my birthright. *Oh Stan!* the charity-ball ladies cried. And he smiled—a gentle indulgent servant's smile, glad to have pleased.

SHE DEALT OUT his glittering rooms, the flash cards of mid-century moments, laid them on the table like a winning poker hand, her smoky voice describing his transient world, without too much socialist realism. Keep the cheating lawyer and the Barefoot Contessa out of it. Stick with his flowers and the flickering candle sconces. Sit on Napoleon, don't forget to dust Benito's claws.

I permitted her to transform our kitchen morning into the ballroom night she had filched from her place at a corner table by the dance floor, a watchful wren perched among the cockatoos. Brief captions below her sharp photographs were also allowed—hadn't she said, *Life is so sad, so sad?* And didn't I feel a thrill of strange recognition?

And by the way, none other than Harmon Hunter III asked her to dance, she reported. A little shrug. So what? No social climber, she. She was just as content to invite the conversation of a drunk who sidled up to us at Mickey's Diner on Wabasha downtown where we stopped for milk shakes after the dentist.

Harmon Hunter sat at her table for a while, had a cigarette with her. Used a cigarette holder, clamped it with his smile, a jutting chin. Like FDR, though of course a damn Republican.

What a beautiful room your husband's given us, he said gallantly. The room was full of roses and pine garlands, cedar and the blue of Noble fir, an unusual combination, as everyone said.

No one will forget this night, he told her.

Another drag on the Tareyton. She gazed off, smiling as she told this.

She was leading me to the room you enter entirely alone, where all the descriptions pile up, where there are no stories and no mistakes. Just pictures, cut like roses, at the height of perfection. Better to stay with the photograph of the scene, before the earthlings mess everything up.

Into this chamber of surface beauty she led me. Or my father led me.

No, it was she with her airy nothings who led the way, not he with the work itself. She with her seraphic smile, off a bit, not smiling at me, her brain-bomb ticking, reaching past us to some room beyond the one she was describing. *Can't you just see it, darling?*

Chapter 3

YEARS AGO, when my parents still lived on Linwood, a writer from Boston came to visit me. She wanted to meet my mother. Tea in the little living room, the two of us sitting on Napoleon, Mother crouched on Benito. Talk about Boston (an Irish city, home of the one Catholic president, heart of American history). And would my friend like to see the Archive?

I stayed downstairs, clearing the dishes, while they went up to my former bedroom, now her office. She had prevailed on my father to build bookcases for her library holdings, the row of Irish history, the collection of biographies of women, the well-marked Flannery O'Connor (*She had the most wonderful relationship with her mother—have you read* The Letters?). My brother was there pictorially in all the stages of his life, serene baby to sweet-faced boy holding out a hot dog with radiant joy at a picnic. High school, college, his wedding, his children, the big fishing trip to Alaska he had arranged for our father.

The rest of the room was devoted to . . . me. She had gathered everything from grade-school papers and birthday cards through book publication, reviews, and articles. Anything, anything. Each item labeled and cataloged.

When we were driving back to my house, my Boston friend looked at me searchingly. "She showed me the refrigerator notes," she said with wonder.

"The refrigerator notes?"

"The Post-its you leave on the refrigerator if you stop over and nobody's there and you say hi, I stopped by. She has them cataloged."

A deep burn of shame, the hopelessness of escape.

"It's a shrine," the woman said. "Amazing." A tone of dismay, a look of barely disguised pity. A terrible family secret she'd stumbled on. We said no more about it.

And now, still here, the spectral Cathedral spaceship out of the hospital window, dark night of her escaping soul. Still holding her hand, still writing her obituary that is also his obituary: when she goes, he's finally gone. A work that will be published widely. Self-published, actually: I'll pay for every word, the longest death notice in *Pioneer Press* memory. The only published page she won't catalog for the Archive.

Even the young funeral director, who tries to steer me to the cherrywood casket with the ruched satin lining and offers the stationery option for the thank-you cards I'll need, even he will be abashed. Just a day from now he'll take the three pages from my hand in his faux-comfy office, and though it can't be said that he *reads* it all, he sifts the pages, his eye reckoning the lines. He's my literary agent for this deal—he'll pass it along to the paper, it's part of the service he provides. He looks up, worry in his eyes. *Could you cut it down some?* he suggests, an editor delicately nudging a chronic overwriter. *It's awful long. Gonna be awful spendy.*

I need every word, I say coldly, and hand the pages back to him. His worried eyes turn to awe.

I know all this because, being the writer, I have no time/ space restrictions. I'm everywhere and of course I'm omniscient. Here at the margin of this last night, note-taking with the eternal yellow legal pad on my lap, stray bits of Celtic clairvoyance allow me to see tomorrow, not to mention a truckload of yesterdays. Magical realism isn't all south of the border. The little people murmur and mutter in the cold. We believed a lot of crazy but true things here in old St. Paul.

We knew the Virgin Mother had appeared to the children at Fatima. At least one of the secrets she conveyed was so horrible that the Pope fainted when he read it. The end of the world was in there, probably. This was the Pope who died of hiccups, which was hysterical but also dead serious in case you started laughing out loud in class thinking of the Bishop of Rome, all in white and gold, hiccupping his way to heaven. *It's not funny, children. Let us pray for our Holy Father.*

We also knew our guardian angel was perched—right there—on our shoulder (left shoulder, heart side). And when you lost anything, you recited over and over:

> St. Anthony, St. Anthony,
> Please come round.
> Something's been lost
> And must be found.

And guess what? You found it. Always. In this way everything lost was always found. Nothing was ever lost. Not in St. Paul. This is why you could never *fall away* from the Church, why you would always be faithful: St. Anthony would keep your stuff safe and sound. And you too. With him and your guardian angel riding shotgun, you'd never experience loss. You were faithful, a daughter of the Church, a toenail on the Mystical Body.

Even pain—physical, mental, you name it, all forms of anguish, misery, any plight or pity, all injustices, losses and humiliations, all the meanness you're likely to encounter in this life (because don't think life will be *easy*, girls and boys)—all of it has a purpose. *Just offer it up*, Mother would say, echoing the nuns. *Offer it up.*

She showered the confidence of eternal life on my brother and me, the best form of solidarity a mother could give a child, cool and impersonal but certain, like her hand holding mine as we walked past Birdie's Market on Wabasha. Now, as an adult, I regard the child-rearing on display in restaurants, the fashionable, preternaturally patient mothers leaning down to their imperious three-year-olds. *Do you want the California roll? No? Would you like the calamari? Sweetie, what would you like?*

Give the kid the mac and cheese and tell him to offer it up. I have become my mother's kind of mother without ever having children.

That's how it is tonight, this night that goes backward (mostly) and forward. I do hope to go forward, but right now I must take this detour of memory. I must *offer it up*. If you can do that, you're free. Free of what? Of sadness—*so sad, so sad?* Or free of *her?* I'm offering it up, here on the eternal ledger of the legal pad. It's our kind of magical realism, angel snug on my shoulder, the Blessed Mother whispering from her bomb-brain because she knows I'm faithful. I'm the daughter of herself and of this place where we believed and believed. It was the way we lived. It wasn't religion. It was poetry.

St. Paul had poetry running in the gutters. Its neighborhoods—Irvine Park, Crocus Hill, Mac Groveland, Ramsey Hill, West Seventh—were marked by the illogic of the city's fierce begetting as a French and Indian fur-trading river town originally named by a half-blind whiskey runner: Pig's Eye. Leo the Lion loved that—*we started as a bar.*

Numbered streets crossed each other fecklessly, as if city planners had used a scribble rather than a grid as a template.

This was nothing like the tidy squaring of numbered avenues and alphabetical street names that Scandinavian Minneapolis laid like a crosshatched veil over the flat features of its city.

The St. Paul streetlights dissipated their glow rather than truly shed it on the crusted snowbanks. This was strangely beguiling—that light could be conscripted into the service of obscurity, a St. Paul trick. In November, the October blaze of elms and maples was finished, and the bleached, beseeching gray bones of the leafless trees were ranked the length of Summit Avenue, going from church to church, past the old mansions. A faint tea-dance violin floated over it all. *Yes*, one of the nuns at my convent school said, *I danced with Scott at the cotillion…*

The damp powder of speakeasy passions and forsaken gangster parties rose from the drenched lilacs in May, and in winter we walked to school through the monastic snow. One of the Irish great-aunts had lived in an apartment on Lexington near Summit for a while. When she moved out, Dillinger moved in. And, my mother delighted in saying, when Dillinger moved out, he moved out shooting. We were proud of our gangster past. Crooks and killers, hoodlums and bank robbers were airbrushed by time, made into lost movie stars from old St. Paul where the cops let them lie low as long as they behaved themselves here.

What a romantic city it was, full of believers, wrapped in pride and insecurity, those protons of provincial complacency. We pulled the blanket of winter around us, we clicked shut the wooden blinds of summer against the killing heat. But our drama was all just weather, the swatted mosquitoes of summer, the dripping ice dams of winter. Our lives were little, our weather big.

A *provincial capital of a middling sort* as I read with unhappy recognition in Gogol during my Russian period in high school. St. Paul was somehow Russian—I sensed that— minus the aristocrats. Or maybe we had those too. We had Summit Avenue, we had Scott Fitzgerald to draw the blood of class consciousness.

St. Paul was so baroquely Catholic that even Lutherans described themselves as being "non-Catholic." St. Paul Jews, when giving their address, might say, if you didn't recognize the street name, "You know, Sacred Heart," indicating a parish boundary. No one thought this odd.

In some cities, the rare lyric ones, alley shadows and the golden clots cast from octagonal streetlights convey light and shade like communiqués to be decoded, their meanings illusive but provocative. Such fragile civic mysteries hold a promise of things to come—though in St. Paul there was always the sense that everything was happening elsewhere. Or that everything had *already* happened. We were living in an aftermath.

But an aftermath of what? Maybe the great robber-baron age that branded Scott Fitzgerald, the brash age that had cast upon the bluffs of the city the beefy Victorian mansions of Summit Avenue. This was our primary proof of (former) greatness—the brooding piles of Summit Avenue from the age of James J. Hill. "The Empire Builder," my father said, always adding this phrase like a royal title that must be accorded the railroad titan, our Carnegie, our Rockefeller.

But his admiration was tinged with regretful disapproval. As a young man in the thirties, he had been union shop steward at the greenhouse. He believed in the common good. He could never quite understand greed or ambition, not even raw entrepreneurial instinct. He preferred to think such things didn't exist or existed only as imprecise abstractions, not pulsing within the human heart. Not in St. Paul. Not in his town, which was his world. Like all big-time qualities, they resided... elsewhere. Not here in the blameless middle.

Never mind. The essential thing was that the world is beautiful—*Look around you!* he would cry, driving us to Lake Minnewashta on Sunday afternoons to go fishing. When he was an old man, he bought a dog, a springer spaniel, the aptly named Buddy, who followed him everywhere with a mournful look on his furrowed brow. They went for rides together in the Buick, the way we did in the Ford after Mass on Sundays.

But Buddy, for all his faithfulness, proved to be a disappointment. He jumped in the car with alacrity, but he immediately stretched out the length of the backseat and slumped his broody head beneath his paws as if he had a migraine and the light were painful to him. "Look at that," my father would say, exasperated. "I take him for a ride—he doesn't even sit up and look at the scenery. Buddy, Buddy—up, up!" My girlhood in the backseat rose before my eyes. *Look, look!*

But the attention my father demanded was a world away from the note-taking watchfulness of my mother in the corners of charity balls. She was tracking. He was filled with wonder. St. Paul provided all the beauty a person needed—St. Paul and an occasional trip into the glory of the Minnesota lake country. Leo the Lion plotted guided trips to Ireland that he argued were a waste of time and money. The Thoreau of St. Paul, he said Europe could wait, he hadn't seen all of Minnesota yet.

The world—that is, St. Paul—was filled with wonders. For him, son of Czech immigrants, graduate of Mechanic Arts High School, and lifelong mourner for the college education he never had, as well as lifelong employee (and finally, well into middle age, joint owner) of the city's best greenhouse, florists to the St. Paul carriage trade over generations from the nineteenth century—for this man, the world was demonstrably a field of good waiting to emerge under the steady care of its watchful tender: himself.

Didn't the world renew itself in annual continuity, sleeping in winter, rising refreshed in spring? Consider the Easter lilies of house number 9. They may neither toil nor spin, but my father toils for them, fostering them under glass and blacklight tarps. The greenhouse, where he spent his days, was an enchanting working replica displaying the world's fundamental mechanics of renewal and reliable cyclical rebirth. Here, at root level, Justice conveyed the inevitable return of life, the security of the organic cycle.

In a way, I was a farm kid, hanging out at the greenhouse,

watching wet baby rabbits slither out of their mother's fur in the dank bulb cellar, or running through the glass houses to the barn where the Christmas trees were stacked, waiting for Charlie, a red-haired giant, to cream them with his flocking gun. Sometimes Charlie gave me jobs: *You go deadhead all those geraniums.* I could keep all the flowers. But my father shook his head—I could keep three or five (always an odd number, odd numbers look better).

I was willing to be enchanted. In spring, I trailed my hand in the black water of the big tank in the far greenhouse, near the barn, where water lilies were kept to stock summer pools. Torpid goldfish, some of them orange, others freakishly spotted like Guernsey cows, all of them immense, lumbered through the dark water, too sinister to be pets. I put my head down low and blew on the water's surface. Nothing disturbed these beasts. Charlie passed by. "They eat them in China," he said, looking down at the fish as he galumphed along in his Wellingtons. An exotic alarm charged my heart.

The greenhouse workforce was composed of older growers who had been immigrants from Central Europe, and younger homeboys who drank beer and belonged to a bowling league. They bought numbers from a bookie for the Saturday Gopher football game. They played 500 for nickels at coffee break. My father smiled indulgently when they swore, and then they apologized to me, blushing to have uttered the S word in the presence of a girl. The F word—there was no F word in the greenhouse. "Clean it up, boys," Charlie would say, when

Rose and Fern, the only female growers, came into the lunchroom from house 10 for coffee.

I don't make up the names. They were Rose and Fern, one from Germany, the other a St. Paul girl bearing the last name of Treewiler as if she descended from a family of climbing vines. Bill Vero, who had trained in Austria, said grace over his meat-loaf sandwich in the lunchroom. His son was a missionary in Madagascar, wherever that was. Chester read the dictionary during lunch break. An odd duck. He complained that the newspaper crossword was too easy. Insulting to a man's intelligence. He belonged to Mensa. *Do you know the meaning of circumnavigation, Patricia? Can you spell it? Ask me any word, ask me how to spell it.*

Everything changed in the design room. This was no farm. Here, where the floral arrangements and corsages and all the funeral and wedding flowers were made up, the demographics and social life moved into the world of decor, the lab for the theatrics of party-giving. Some of the male designers, young and slim, wore pastel angora sweaters. They told me, as I sat on a high stool watching them work, that my father was the *handsomest* man. They came, they went, but always, during the late fifties and sixties of my girlhood, the cloudy angora sweaters abounded, a blush of color at the cheekbone, the flutter of mascara at the lash. They called me honey, not an endearment the silent growers in the greenhouse ever used at their solitary benches, potting seedlings.

Occasionally my father would ask someone to cut back

on the eye shadow. But in general, it was understood: these were people of talent, more talent than the average person could hope to possess. Artists. You want something really *nice*, this is where you go. This is the person you want for your daughter's wedding, for your father's casket spray. "Make it special, won't you, Dickie?" the Crocus Hill ladies cooed, claiming personal privilege with a top designer.

It was known that the designers held crazy parties. They got drunk and cried. Once I heard my father say "cocaine" with a deep frown. It was the early sixties and the word suggested jazz rather than addiction like other words of indulgence—sauna, massage, martini. I coveted the angora sweaters and awaited the breathless semi-confidences I was sometimes awarded just for sitting there, watching a corsage come into existence from deft fingers twirling green florist tape, pinkie ring flashing.

Sometimes there were sighs over slights and injustices of the weekend before. Black eyes and crashing headaches in the design room. "What a night! My *head*!" Dickie would say, hinting at much, offering little in the way of detail. "Honey, be a doll, go down to the machine and get me a Coke? I *need* a Coke. *God*." Such tribulations were clear indicators of the artistic temperament. I scurried off to the lunchroom Coke machine to do what I could in the way of stress relief.

THE BOILER ROOM was a place apart. Strange—the boiler room refuses to locate itself exactly in my mental blueprint of the greenhouse. But somewhere near the garage area where the delivery trucks were kept, I see my father opening a door. I follow him. We are standing on a metal grating. Below us— for the whole of the room exists in a sudden drop under this metal gallery—the big vault of the enclosure is taken up with a massive seething boiler. Down there, on a folding chair propped against the far wall at an angle, sits a man wearing suspenders over a ribbed undershirt. I know who he is: the night watchman, a term fraught with alarm. It is he who sometimes calls in the middle of the night to say the boiler has gone out. In winter this is the Worst Thing that can happen. The boiler is a raging god. Its raging must never stop.

At the sight of my father, the man snaps his chair back in place. He has been sleeping. There is a bottle of Grain Belt next to the chair. He is supposed to be awake. The Grain Belt is wrong, too. We go down the steep metal steps to the dirt floor where the watchman is now standing. The roar of the boiler is so loud my father has to shout. The night watchman shouts, too. Yet they are not angry at each other. They're conferring, but I don't understand what they're saying. The heat pulses from the giant jelly roll of the boiler. The watchman opens the little door. He and my father bend down to look. The heat surges hungrily forward, groaning. Hell is in there. Hell is red but also white. I must not let on how scary it is or my father won't bring me back. That's strange: it's awful yet it would be more awful not to be able to return here. I'm consumed by contradiction. It's wonderful, this terrible place.

When we leave, I'm shocked that we're leaving the night watchman behind. It isn't safe in that room with the heat panting. I ask my father why we're leaving him there. "It's his job," he says. "He has to stay."

All of this—my father's world and therefore mine—is inevitable, the only way things can be. The alien goldfish move in black water in their tin tank somewhere near the geranium house. Do they sleep? Do they swim as they sleep? Terrible oddities abrade our peaceful world. We are not exempt. I was born here, a block from the greenhouse on Banfil, street of Czech immigrants. Big kitchen gardens, much canning of tomatoes in summer. In the fall people laid out damp mushrooms to dry on window screens set across sawhorses. They knew which ones you could eat, which would kill you. The lore of forests. We called our landlady "Teta"—Auntie. Everyone seemed related. It took me a while to sort out who the real aunts were from the honorary ones.

Though we have moved away from Banfil, up to Linwood, this is my place, the dark apartment on Banfil where Teta still lives (she works holidays at the greenhouse). We've moved "up the hill." We've bought a house, a bungalow where Napoleon and Benito sit along with mild Mr. Williams. "I just know we can make the monthly, Mary," my eager father says to my frowning mother who has always lived in an apartment, and until she married never had a bedroom.

Home ownership, she felt, was overrated. But necessary—the children apparently had to have a house. Child-rearing was a mystery, years deferring to my father whose oldest sister eloped at sixteen and was widowed at twenty, coming home with three small children. He was an uncle at nine, all of them living in the house near the brewery. *Your father knew about babies, he knew what to do.*

Whereas she had slept on the davenport in the living room of the Marshall Street apartment, next to the Irish grandmother who could neither read nor write but spoke to the little people. The grandmother died of cancer of the nose, an awful little pink pineapple emerging from a nostril, and then she was dead. It would be better to be the Pope and die of hiccups, better than dying of a tiny pineapple in your nose.

I understood that the little house on Linwood was a move up. St. Paul with its hierarchical topography underscored the point: below on the flats were the poor, the newly arrived; above on the bluff the rich and the rising. I understood we were rising, a bit anyway. I was not glad. I didn't understand why we had left Banfil, left Teta and the wizening mushrooms that Teta says are delicious and my mother won't let us eat. *Say thank you. Flush them down the toilet.*

Banfil is the old world, as my Czech grandmother speaks of Bohemia, where she came from. She doesn't write English. That's shameful but we pretend it doesn't matter. She worked as housekeeper for a Supreme Court Justice. Yes! The United States Supreme Court. The Justice came home in the summer because he wanted her soup. He said that. Nothing

Soup, it was called. She's a great cook. She thinks my mother and I read too much (*bad for the eyes, bad*).

We have emigrated the little but decisive vertical distance from Banfil to Linwood. My father wants this. He will not allow my mother an herb garden. We'll have roses, he says, and geraniums and impatiens in the shaded window boxes. Vegetables and herbs were for West Seventh, *down there*. It was as if he thought a kitchen garden wasn't *allowed* "up the hill."

Yet he never really left, never quite made the leap that was somehow more unbridgeable than the ocean the Czech grandmother and grandfather crossed. They jumped to the New World and never looked back.

But he goes back every day to the greenhouse, and we buy our groceries at Johnson and Johnson Market on West Seventh. Why is it called Johnson and Johnson when it's owned by Mr. Schoner and Mr. Goldman? Where are the Johnsons?

There are no Johnsons. Mr. Schoner and Mr. Goldman are Jewish, so they call it Johnson and Johnson.

Why do they do that?

It's better for business.

Oh.

Mr. Goldman says I'm a chatterbox and he likes a talker. He hands me a Hershey bar. I'm stabbed with regret: I have to say no, it's Lent. We don't eat candy in Lent. *I'll save it for you*, he says, smiling, taking it back. I feel the little bumps of almond under the wrapper as the bar leaves my hand. But Mr. Goldman forgets. He never offers it again. I have the gift of gab and a silent ache for sugar.

We belong to this.

My father stayed at the greenhouse, near the little houses with the kitchen gardens, working on the flats where the greenhouses were built sometime late in the nineteenth century, about the time his own mother and father arrived from Bohemia. He never strayed far from the Gothic towers of Schmidt Brewery where his brother, Frankie, was scalded to death in the Depression, a freak industrial accident.

We leave the hellish boiler room. We step into the dry ice of winter. Orion's big X, the winter constellation, marks the north. We go to the car—a Ford Fairlane. That's another step up, fins and owly headlights, two-tone white and green, the same green as the greenhouse trucks, the rich green of healthy foliage. My father unlocks my door first, the passenger side, a winter courtesy, then goes around to his door.

In spite of the paradisal work of summer he is consigned to do, winter is his true home, a place both real and imaginary. Just as the terror I bring from the boiler room's edge of hell is real and yet it's also something I've made up to scare myself. Lucky my guardian angel's there, barest weight on my left shoulder, looking out for me.

The hellish boiler room fires the cool blossoms in the glass houses, the winter sky wheels above us when we step outside and are smacked with cold. It's all inevitable, marvelous—*Beautiful*, my father says crossing to the driver's side of the Fairlane, taking in a deep draft of our coldness, head cocked up to the navy sky, *Just look at those stars.*

HE ADORED WINTER, and referred to the god-awful Minnesota cold as "a change of season." He wore a London Fog when it was twenty below zero, and felt sorry for Southern Californians, people limited to a year-round Mediterranean climate. On a rare visit to Los Angeles he ordered a fruit salad, and was served a bowl of syrupy cubed peaches and wan grapes *from a can.* "We get their fresh fruit," he said, as if California were best understood as a supply colony for Minnesota.

Even more wonderful than the renewal of life that the refreshing Minnesota change of seasons bestowed on us was the urban farm of the greenhouse where he seduced and betrayed the calendar and the clock and of course the climate, timing blossoms as if with a stopwatch for the holidays, Christmas poinsettias and Easter lilies hoodwinked and hustled, duped and drugged, depending on their growth cycles, so they all bloomed for his customers exactly on the dot. The white clappers of lilies, still closed on Palm Sunday, opened promptly on Easter morning from their bladelike stems, glistening with well-timed resurrection.

There we are on the great church holidays—Mother, Father, Peter, me—in the oak pews of St. Luke's, admiring the stage set of the sanctuary, always lushly over-the-top thanks to my father, grander than the altar decorations at St. Mark's or

Holy Spirit. He donated and arranged it all under the massive frieze portrait of Jesus that dominated the sanctuary. Our Jesus was dark and Byzantine, beckoning East. He bestowed on us a slight Giaconda proto-smile of the sort art historians puzzle over. He reclined against a bright blue–fringed bolster, spangled with bewitching gold stars, the sort of bedchamber pillow the French Orientalists used to outfit their fantasias of the seraglio.

This was not the crucified Christ, though his open hands displayed tidy, decorative stigmata. Ours was the Jesus who suffered instead the perfumed oils of the Magdalene, a large hearted Lord lingering at table with his friends, the holy man who chose, for his first miracle, to make more wine. A generous host with no time for church bean counters fretting that too many flowers in the sanctuary sent the wrong message when, from the pulpit, the priest announced a second collection for the heating fund.

During one benighted period, St. Luke's had a timorous pastor who told my father he'd better cut back on the Christmas decorations. The masses of poinsettias and the clumps of Fraser firs my father had sketched on his master plan as backdrop for the manger scene were...well, too much.

Too much? What on earth could that mean? What about John, chapter 12? *Then Mary brought a pound of very costly perfume, pure oil of nard, and anointed Jesus' feet and wiped them with her hair, till the house was filled with the frag-*

rance. It was Judas, we recalled, who protested against this indulgence.

Nor did we take kindly to the dreary "memorials preferred" directive, tacked at the end of small-minded death notices in the *Pioneer Press.* "In lieu of flowers!" my father would exclaim as he read the paper at the breakfast table.

He appealed to my brother and me, asking us to consider *our* funeral wishes. "Wouldn't you rather have a beautiful display of flowers?" he asked, looking for confirmation of the right values of the world. We nodded loyally over our oatmeal—definitely, we'd take the flowers over the check for cancer research.

"I mean, cancer research, sure," he would say magnanimously, willing to meet medical science halfway, "but you have to have flowers." Love and flowers, death and flowers. But flowers, flowers, always flowers, the insignia of death, the hope of resurrection.

YET HE WAS NOT wholly content. Unlike the older growers, men who had been trained in the conservatories of Austria and Germany in the late nineteenth century, and then, via the seignorial gardens of Cuba and Argentina, had made their improbable way to the modest but secure potting benches of the Banfil Street greenhouse in St. Paul where they worked with monastic absorption, my father had a bright Summit Avenue eye.

He may have been born on West Seventh, beneath the shadow of the Schmidt Brewery where his prizefighter older brother, the glamorous Frankie, died his horrible death before he was thirty. And he may have worked at the greenhouse "down there" all his life, but he looked up, up. The backsides of the Summit Avenue mansions crowned the bluff directly above the greenhouse. It was to these back doors that he tended.

He looked up, but not out. Yet one feverish season—I must have been ten—there was wild talk over the dinner table about moving to a rhododendron ranch in Argentina. We would leave St. Paul—imagine! My alluring father, with his sweep of dark hair and aquiline nose, would wear chaps and ride herd over the rhododendrons. A floral gaucho in a silver-studded weskit and a ten-gallon hat. I would have a spotted pony. Great World, here we come.

Soon after this flurry of excitement, he bought the full World Book encyclopedia from a neighbor who had been lobbying him to sign up for a set. My brother had been given a pocketknife for his birthday and was irresistibly drawn to this woman's garden hose and methodically cut through the green rubber in tidy six-inch intervals, like the meticulous surgeon he would later become. The least we could do was cave in and buy the World Book from her at last.

For years at night before bed my father took a volume off the shelf, reading at random about far-flung places and moments in history, scientific discoveries, and wild beasts. Fiji and Bhutan, Napoleon on Elba, Einstein and Freud, the gar fish, the hundred-year aloe. It's how he ended his day, roaming the world. But the World stayed in its Book. And we stayed in St. Paul, playing the geographic card we'd been dealt.

THE DEPRESSION, unlike dreams of escape, remained a destination of another sort in our postwar household, a still-potent explanation for just about every life choice, every disappointment or lack. Because of the Depression, my father had not gone to college (I was forty before it occurred to me that *some* people had gone to college during the Depression). Because of the Depression he had not become a doctor or an architect (his two alternate lives). Because of the Depression he had stayed at the greenhouse, glad of the job.

And because of the Depression he worked like a dog—but this was Leo the Lion talking, looking up from her two-inch-thick history of the Irish, shaking her head over her husband, happiest of workaholics. "I've never had to worry about another woman," she would say. "That greenhouse is his mistress." And back she would go to *her* true love, the endless pages demonstrating the egregious humiliations the English had inflicted over centuries upon the Irish. In her ancestral mind, she was always crouched in a hedgerow school in Kilkenny, the peat fires smoldering. Compared to the Famine and the Troubles, the Depression was amateur night in the annals of anguish.

My father was incapable of her Irish grudges. For him,

history's darkness belonged to the Depression, and he held on to it. He even suggested that because of the Depression, Frankie had been killed, Frankie who was still hoping to make it big on the welter-weight circuit. He had lost a good black-smithing job to the Depression and had only been doing pickup work at the brewery on that terrible day in early May. "The tulips had just opened," he would say thoughtfully, as if even then he clocked all events of import in floral time.

But—and here was the paradoxical kicker to it all—also "because of the Depression" people had lived together in an enchanted circle, happy. "Nobody had *anything*," he would say, his voice rising in crescendo when he spoke of his youth and the early years of his marriage. When nobody had any-thing, my brother and I were led to believe, universal har-mony had prevailed on earth.

Unlike Dexter Green, Scott Fitzgerald's hero in "Winter Dreams," a St. Paul story, who did not just want "association with glittering things and glittering people—he wanted the glittering things themselves," my father did not aspire to wealth. He did not crave "the glittering things themselves." His mother, like Dexter's, "was a Bohemian of the peasant class" and she too "talked broken English to the end of her days." But my father didn't try for a Summit Avenue heart-breaker the way Dexter chose—and lost—Judy Jones. He married his high-school girl and stuck with her. He never abandoned the friends or habits of his working-class youth, he didn't become rich, and money didn't seem to be the engine stoking his winter dreams.

He was not what is called a good businessman. It wasn't that he was careless or wasteful or gambled unwisely—except for the rash act of eventually buying the greenhouse from those who had left it sagging with the debt of ages. It was a three-generation family business, moving inexorably down the hereditary chain from the grim hardworking founders, to the two-martini-lunch middle generation until it foundered finally in the vain trust-fund expectations of the smooth-talking third generation. My father served them all in turn from youth deep into middle age.

He wasn't shrewd. His business talents were those of a faithful retainer, fatally steadfast, dedicated, a believer in surfaces, a truster of the good word of others. And as my mother maintained from her elevated perch of Irish mistrust, he admired the rich. A Fitzgeraldian fault that perhaps came with the Summit Avenue territory.

The greenhouse was his love. There was something dangerous in loving your work too much. Such passion betrayed the ruinous appetite of an artist. And weren't the lives of artists cautionary rather than exemplary tales? Stay away from all that.

But he never thought of himself as an artist.

Too bad. It might have helped, in the end, had he allowed himself that small, saving vanity.

Chapter 4

It's TIME TO LOOK at the picture. Not a photograph. Later we'll look at more photographs, the way every family does, making much of the frozen moments, the icons of ancestry, the dead laughing right in your face, or just staring that noncommittal historical gaze. And before this is over I'll have to pick a photograph of Leo the Lion for her obit in the *Pioneer Press*. I have one in mind. But that can wait.

It's the oil painting I'm hauling out in the dark of her last room, propping it up in my mind. The painting I have at home. I can't say, "The one hanging on the wall at home." It's in a closet, faced to the back wall.

My father took up painting when he retired. In spite of his passion for his work, in spite of the lifelong habit of it, he did retire. Heart attacks and money worries, cheats and bad luck—I'll get to that. But he had to quit. That's when he took up the violin. And he started painting. No surprise, his subject was usually floral, meticulously articulated African violets, seven-foot-tall iris and alstroemeria on panels for a display at the State Fair. But we don't need to look at those. The one in the closet is the only one I need to drag out tonight, the only one to consider.

It has a title: *Patricia's Garden.* He had a little brass label made and engraved with these words. Small round-head rivets attach the brass to the picture frame. The painting hung on their living-room wall till he died. Then my mother said I should have it. Which is when it went into the closet. I told her I was waiting to find the perfect place for it. But I had found the perfect place. It's possible she understood that.

A sweet picture, comic in a way, and I should get a kick out of it, make a joke, be done with it. But a burn rises when I look at the smear of pastel that is me and my alleged garden. A wall in the background is mossed over, climbing with vines and dabs of flowers the color of fondant. The garden my father provides me with is a convent garden. I recognize the look—didn't they send me to a girls' school to be taught by cloistered nuns? A bench is angled in the foreground, a big tub of cabbage roses at one end. Pretty, pretty.

On this bench sits Miss Muffet, the me-myself of my father's fond illusion, small feet shod in ballet slippers, neatly crossed at the ankle, barely peeking out from the long dress. A white dress—ohmygod, now that I'm actually considering it, I see it's none other than the Scarlett O'Hara wedding dress, the choker collar, the flounces on the skirt. I'm wearing a big straw hat too, a garland of flowers weighing it down low on my demure brow, ribbon streamers down the back. And in my hand? A wee book I regard mildly, must be a book of poesy. Or my mother's bridal prayer book fragrant with flowers.

So what's the problem? Why is the painting stuffed in the closet? Who am I afraid I am? Not Leo the Lion (the shaded face belongs to no one), not Scarlett O'Hara, in spite of the dress. If only I could say I have been a Scarlett O'Hara.

The problem, doctor, is that this person sitting on her tuffet in her bower of flowery bliss, bound in her virginal dress, gazing at her teeny-tiny poems—this girl's never going to escape. She's going nowhere. She's her father's angel, her mother's dutiful daughter. She's staying till it's over. An indentured innocent. Everything is contrived—the vines and blossoms, the wall high as a monastic enclosure, the constricting obscuring dress, and the gaze trained on the itty-bitty bookette—it's the hex of love.

The Great World, the world of *filth*, the high jinks of the arty outlaw life—it's never going to happen to you, girlfriend. Just look at yourself. Take a good long look during this last night of your life as a daughter, your time as their girl. Beneath the feminist posturing, the difficult boyfriends, the lefty politics, the gallant travels "behind the Iron Curtain" (the boldest destination I could think of, imprisoned land of the Czech side of the family), behind the poetry writing, I was the virgin daughter attending to her ailing parents.

No wonder I adored all those nineteenth-century novels—
I was living one.

MY FATHER WISHED UPON ME a virginity whose innocence
was only dimly related to sex. It went deeper and flooded the
whole reservoir of the soul with freshets of trust, pools of willing dependence. He wished me to be ethereal, untouched by
the world and its dingy habits, its money-mind.

"Do you know if we're rich or poor?" he asked abruptly one
day when I was in high school. We were in the green-and-white
finned Ford sedan. He was taking me to school in the morning,
a private Catholic school beyond our means, the one extravagance of their lives: the education of my brother and me.

"No," I said truthfully. I didn't know the difference between $2,000 and $200,000.

But the question was unsettling.

"Good," he said, his priestly face steady on the road, not
looking at me. Just checking. Glad things were in order, my
ignorance safely intact as if it were my honor. And his.

Do we live paycheck to paycheck? I asked my mother a
while later. It was a phrase I had heard at school, and I could
not think what was on the other side of that equation.

Of course, she said to this mad question.

Are we poor? I asked searchingly, sensing that paychecks
had to do with the question my father did not want me to be
able to answer.

No, she said.

Are we rich?

No!—this delivered with emphatic pride, as if to be poor might be bad luck, but being rich was disreputable.

Never worry about money, she said with fine disdain, an Irish heiress bankrolled by pride alone.

It was about the time he decided to take up the offer the owners were making to risk everything and buy the flower business. *Never worry about money.* We both knew, Mother and I, that he worried about just that.

ONE OF THE FEW TIMES he lashed out at me was the day I came home from the University and in answer to his usual question—*what had I learned today*—I told him that in Economics the lecture had been on planned obsolescence. My brother was in dentistry school, preparing to do something useful. But I was an English major, sitting around reading poetry and novels and picking up fancy ideas. Dad was beginning to see me as a sort of human World Book, a trove of random info—didn't I spend the day studying this and that, one term taking Early Kievan Russian History, the next careening over to Cultural Anthropology.

I explained that manufacturers *arranged* for their goods—cars, nylon stockings—to break down. Leo the Lion was nodding—made sense to her. The point, I explained, was that people have to buy and buy, in a continuing cycle, thus keeping the whole market economy aloft on the wings of prearranged need. A plot, really.

"Do you mean to tell me," he said, putting down his fork, "that all the money the floral industry has spent on research to hybridize a poinsettia that will last the whole Christmas season—and beyond, well beyond into spring so that some people wish they *would* die—that we're trying to make the flowers *wither* so people will buy more?" He looked affronted. "It's a lie." He glared at me as if I had tarnished his reputation.

I couldn't talk him down from the good intentions of the floral industry back to the guile of the free market concepts I was absorbing from the big Samuelson text I lugged back and forth to the University. He was personally offended by the concept of planned obsolescence, betrayed by this University education he was providing his hard-hearted daughter.

The sharpness that apparently came with a University education, the cold satisfactions of the intellectual hunt—he hadn't counted on this. The University wasn't, after all, like paging through the World Book after a long day at the greenhouse, the exhausting weight of labor lightened by one illuminating and uplifting fact after another. Getting an education was something else altogether—darker. And unkind.

MY MOTHER, with her remorseless Irish eye, had a point: my father was an innocent (a polite word for fool). He did "admire the rich." The word *gentleman* carried a sacred charge for him. He wasn't a snob, he was (the Fitzgeraldian flaw again) a believer. He admired the rococo taste of the dowagers of Summit Avenue and Crocus Hill. They maintained a grandeur he approved of. They were doing their bit, keeping up appearances. And appearance, for him, was not a superficial matter. Decor was not, for him, "decorative," nothing of that insulting diminishment attended it.

The matrons of Summit, the "real ones," the wives and daughters of men whose names meant something in St. Paul—railroad heiresses and other grandees like the founders of 3M—they too believed in the look of things. It was for them he toiled. Or for the idea they held in common. The idea of loveliness. Together they made possible the improbable but necessary presence of exotic, tropical flowers in our killer northland. For we didn't just live in the Midwest—ours was the Upper Midwest, as if we had bypassed the regular Midwest and achieved a Siberian ascendancy that gave us a transcendent existence amid the boreal forests and silent stars.

His lady customers, usually older, often widows, invited him for tea in the late afternoon to discuss their garden plans. Rarely, but memorably, there would be a younger hungry one like the Barefoot Contessa who offered a martini and the information that her husband was out of town on business. He reported these incidents at the dinner table as a joke, a modest boast on the edge of it. Out of town on monkey business, he'd say, and we would laugh, even Mother who seemed to relinquish the power of good looks to him. Such women were "characters," not to be taken seriously. Rich and crazy and spoiled. You had to laugh at them. Pick up your clipboard and start measuring the perennial border. As my mother confidently said, he already had a mistress.

He advised all these ladies on the next growing season, the next party, walking around their property with his clipboard, counting out arbor vitae hedges, warning against swimming pools (people get the strangest ideas, he said at home after talking someone on Kenwood Parkway down from a swimming pool), counting up the number of rental tables a wedding dinner would require, the height of the centerpieces, the advisability of garlanding the sconces, the wisdom of candles versus votive lights, the possibility of velvet roping.

One of his favorite Summit Avenue customers, something of a recluse, had a whole seventeenth-century mirrored room from a Loire castle crated up, and installed on her second floor. "It looks okay," he said laconically. He usually frowned on extremism. He once refused, on ethical grounds, or perhaps aesthetic ones, to flock a Christmas tree black for a customer too stylish for his own good. In the seventies, he did not allow the greenhouse to sell Mylar balloons. "What adult wants a balloon with a bouquet?" he said, though the younger designers tried to explain that balloons were big. There was something almost political about his attempt to foster the best: art (and we had no doubt his work was art) was life's underdog. It needed someone to stand up for it against the bully forces of uncaring and plastic.

The ladies of the little curving streets of leafy Crocus Hill could trust him to follow them in their decorative plots and plans. They called on him to supply the palette of their spring gardens, planted every fall, and then furiously dug up and discarded to be replaced with annuals every summer for a few short months until the whole business had to be rooted out and the process started again. He was impatient with the parsimonious blooming habits of perennials. He used them as a backdrop for the big pop and splash of annuals. His prodigal use of impatiens, in particular, betrayed him as a Fauve, boldly casting purple and orange, shocker pink and violet in wild jots in the shade gardens of Lincoln and St. Clair.

The company's forest-green trucks trolled the streets of the city, doling out the company's narrow powder-pink boxes with the gold logo. Inside, blood-dark long-stem roses, wrapped in waxy green florist paper, lay in grave repose, a severe insignia of Eros.

There were square corsage boxes for evening parties, double-wrapped gift plants, and tiered centerpieces trailing ivy and damask roses, arriving just before the dinner guests, the driver rushing up to the front door, wearing the jacket and cap of the greenhouse, the same logo scrolled over his heart as upon the box he delivered.

Before holidays, the workforce tripled. The whole family— my brother and I, our aunts and cousins—spent long hours in the greenhouse or the downtown shop. Only Leo the Lion steered clear. She'd found a job as a file clerk at a college library, never trusting the illusions of the flower industry, putting her faith in the other dream industry of books.

The extra women employees were set up at a table to "trim" the plants before they were sent out. The clay pot of every poinsettia and azalea, every gloxinia and lily had to be wrapped in stretchy paper, affixed with two straight pins (we had pins sticking out of our mouths but we managed to keep talking with a James Cagney droop to the lip). Then we lavished a bright bow to a wooden stake and drove the stake into the damp earth of the pot so the plant appeared to be wearing a floppy bow tie at its rippled paper collar. We were firm believers in gilding the lily.

Occasionally there was trouble with a customer, but this was usually with the younger matrons, earnest chairwomen of various St. Paul charity events. My father reported on them at the dining-room table, stabbing his fork into the meat loaf as he inveighed against the forces of bad taste.

Late October, and he has just come from meeting with the chairwoman of the annual St. Joseph Hospital Charity Ball. Every year it is a different chairwoman, but it is always the same complaint. This woman—she may as well be singular—has said, as the woman last year also said, and as the chairwoman next year will say, "Stan, I want to do something really *original* this year."

His frustration was wholly philosophical. He liked the woman, he loved the work. But he attacked the meat loaf, saying these people didn't understand anything. What was the point of originality? What on earth did they think they were after? "Do they want me to put the tables upside down and hang the chairs from the ceiling?" he asked as my mother and brother and I shook our heads along with him.

He waited all his life for the chairwomen of the world to admit that beauty had rules, was a unity and not a bunch of random gestures, and that elegance was a matter of classic, indisputable forms.

STANISLAUS RUDOLF (the middle name for his mother's favorite brother, shot in Bohemia for poaching on the noble's estate, such a feudal crime)—Stan to his customers—didn't even desire, I think, proximity to the glittering things that Fitzgerald's Dexter Green with his floral name longed for. His own idea of heaven was the cabin he'd nailed together from greenhouse scrap lumber along a feeder river in the wild-rice fields of northern Minnesota. A guy could relax there, a guy could fish.

Yet he provided these glittering things, devotedly, to several generations of St. Paul matrons. He wanted a certain kind of formal, purchased beauty to *exist*, and especially for this elegance to *mean* something—something good, something hopeful. It was important to him that all this *be* there—the big Crocus Hill houses with their well-thought-out gardens, their holiday parties festooned with out-of-season cut flowers, the stony façades of Summit Avenue mansions draped in

Noble fir branches he expertly twisted around wires to make looping, beribboned garlands. This surface loveliness was *the outward and visible sign*, as the nuns taught us about the sacraments, of an *inward and spiritual grace*, the communion of civic good he believed in, the market economy as sacramental rite.

Another indelible image of him, another framed memory-shot that seems to cancel that exasperated one with the charity-ball women. This time he's not at home. He's in the design room, just off the first greenhouse where all the shiny green plants are kept. He's holding a knife, the pocketknife every florist has in his pocket at all times, the knife that is never loaned to anyone else.

It must be a Sunday afternoon. The greenhouse is closed, the design room silent. He's getting something ready, no doubt for a funeral or the early-Monday hospital delivery round. I'm sitting on the stool by the design table, as I always do, just watching.

He emerges from the walk-in cooler with an armload of flowers—tangerine roses and purple lisianthis, streaked cymbidium orchids, brassy gerbera daisies and little white stephanotis, lemon leaf, trailing sprengeri fern, branches of this, stems of that. He tosses the whole business on the big table, and stands in front of what looks like a garbage heap. An empty vase is set in front of him. He appears to ignore it. He just stands there, his pocketknife in his hand, but not moving, and not appearing to be thinking. He doesn't touch the mess of flowers, doesn't sort them. He just stares for a long vacant minute. He's forgotten I'm sitting there.

Then, without warning, he turns into a whirlwind. Without pause, grabbing and cutting, placing and jabbing, he puts all the flowers into the vase, following some inner logic so that—as people always said of his work—it looks as if the flowers had met and agreed to position themselves in the only possible way they should be. He worked faster than anyone else in the shop, without apparent thought or planning. I could distinguish his arrangements—but they weren't anything as artificial as an "arrangement"—from across the room from the dozens lined up on the delivery table for the truck drivers.

He learned the basics of greenhouse work from the old European growers, people with names strangely apropos to the business: Herman Schoen, an elfin man who looked like a dwarf in *Snow White* but whose name, my father told me, meant "beautiful" in German. Also, the inseparable middle-aged growers, Fern and Rose, solid as farmhands with bright apple cheeks. Their husbands, we understood, occasionally beat them up. One or the other would come to work with a black eye or bruised arm from time to time. Rose's husband came to the greenhouse in lederhosen, the moss-colored leather shorts and cheery folk embroidery seeming sinister and unsettling, given the blackened eyes of his wife. The elderly men growers were courtly with Fern and Rose. "No, no, no," tiny Herman Schoen would cry when Fern, who was taller than he and considerably younger, tried to carry a flat of cuttings to her potting table.

Flower arranging, however, my father learned from two Nisei women who came to Minnesota during the war. They had fled inland from California to avoid Japanese American internment, and my father hired them. For years afterwards they sent us handmade cards at Christmas. They enlisted him, apparently, in the aesthetic of organic form, following the line of the stem. Not for him displays of gladioli arrayed like stiff semaphores in papier-mâché baskets. He would sometimes produce a surprisingly seductive arrangement using only white flowers—by turns flimsy and then juicy, moving from the barest edge of peach to cream and then sheering off to the green of pooled water. The whole composition filled your eye with the unexpected ardor of that virginal color.

He was caught in opposing values. On the one hand, he held the belief, amounting to a religious faith, that there is an underlying something—a law, a rule, an innate recognition of rightness—that exists within matter itself and is understood as elegance. It is not something we make but something we reveal—or even acquiesce to when it is revealed to us. This is my father stabbing furiously at the meat loaf, inveighing against the voice of the world's chairwomen demanding originality.

On the other hand, he stands at the ready with his pocket-knife, just gazing at the welter of cut stems. Then slashing and cutting, jabbing in a perfectly wild, even dangerous way, taking whatever is at hand, finding a place for all of it. This is spontaneity; trust in the face of choice, buoyancy at the edge of chaos. Here, alone in the design room, he appears to be on the side of the demons of originality, not the angels of order.

He was by nature a quiet man, victim of a youthful stutter he had inherited from his father, but had somehow trained into submission. Unlike Mother adrift in her *airy nothings*, he was happier outside of language—in a November duck blind, summers in a fishing boat, or on Lake Milles Lacs ice fishing, just sitting there. Or here in the greenhouse design room on a Sunday afternoon. He brought this silence, an aura of quiet, to the flowers he arranged.

But he didn't arrange them. It was himself he arranged, standing at the ready, sharp knife moving over his materials lightly, surely, like a Japanese ink brush.

Chapter 5

JUST LIKE DOWNTOWN. Aunt Lillian, Frankie's shy, surviving twin sister, said this of anything so marvelous, so luxe that its descriptive requirements billowed beyond superlatives. Something really wonderful had to be awarded high-end real estate. My agoraphobic aunt who rarely left home gave us what became our family's metaphor for the sublime. *Just like downtown.* A curious figure of speech for a woman terrified of leaving the house except in the company of her husband, the big, bluff Bill. But it was a good metaphor for the yearning of the provincial heart.

The flower company's retail shop at Fifth and St. Peter did exist in a zone of glamour, except it wasn't *just like* downtown—it *was* downtown, a world away from the workaday greenhouse on Banfil near the immigrant houses and their cottage gardens.

The store's big window displays, changed by my father by

the month or to suit the season, weren't in St. Paul as we were in St. Paul and as the greenhouse was. The downtown store conveyed a fugitive air of New York—maybe even Paris—that had strayed somehow to the block of shops curving past the St. Paul Hotel. It was directly across the street from Bullard's Jewelers whose haughty display windows were small peepholes that enticed and yet kept you at a distance.

Bullard's was like church—hushed, mysterious, trafficking in jewels and sterling silver that were emblems of transcendence. You couldn't imagine *shopping* at Bullard's. But at least a person could buy a rose now and then. The flower shop, for all its élan, was not unapproachable like Bullard's where every night the riches were squirreled away in vaults like money in a bank. At closing time the little squares of Bullard's windows were emptied. The windows of the flower shop kept their displays through the night, floral sentries on the street of "fine shops."

Next door to Bullard's was Gokey's. Here Theodore Roosevelt and Ernest Hemingway had ordered their *bottes sauvages*, the knee-high snakebite-resistant boots worn by knowing men of action. From here the likewise celebrated Gokey Indian Dressing was sent *around the globe*, as my mother said, to those wishing to protect their leather goods from the dryness of deserts or the rot of jungles. "Gokey's is international," she said with rare earnestness, indicating a step well beyond downtown.

She never said anything was "just like downtown," to her

a moronic remark. She considered my aunt a silly woman, though a good cook. *Well, that's all she does,* Leo the Lion pronounced. *She never leaves the house.* With all that time on my aunt's hands, my mother couldn't see why she didn't read a book now and again. *Your aunt's not much of a reader,* she said. For her, a severe judgment. And Lillian had not been reeled back into the Church, as my mother had managed with my father. "I live by the Golden Rule," Lillian said. There was a department store downtown called the Golden Rule, across the street from one called the Emporium. A mystifying religion, I thought, but Lillian was definitely the best-dressed woman in the family, so who knew?

The flower shop took up a broad swath of the south side of Fifth directly across from Bullard's and Gokey's. There it displayed itself like an exotic beauty propped between the luxurious bolsters of Frank Murphy (the best women's clothes in the city where my mother wouldn't *think* of going) and Field-Schlick (second best—with a lending library she sighed to join though she couldn't justify the membership fee).

People—women especially—paused before my father's big window displays, gazing at the orchids and flowering ginger in *cachepots,* evidence of Hawaii and Costa Rica right there inside as they shivered on the January sidewalk. Their faces were wistful—who could afford all this? Much later, when I traveled to Eastern Europe during the Cold War, I recognized this same soft pang, a reverent longing on the faces of people in Prague who stood in front of sausage shops.

The greenhouse, on the flats of West Seventh, was an indoor farm with none of this ritz. The growers wore overalls and clomped between the raised potting tables in rubber boots, splashing hoses around and muddying the ground beneath the vast mullioned-window roofs. The greenhouse design room was a charmless space off one wing, piled with cheap vases and spools of green wire for strengthening stems. A deep metal sink, ringed with calcium deposits, held tin buckets of mums and glads waiting their turn in the funereal papier-mâché baskets stacked on the floor.

Though the greenhouse had something called a showroom, it was dim and pointless. A barely lit cooler ran along one wall; opposite, the windows gave onto the working-class neighborhood. Banfil, street of my birth, byway of first memories, frost stars on winter windows, iris beaten down by spring rain, Teta's dried mushrooms, food of the fairytale woods. In no way was it *just like downtown.*

It looked as if nobody had dusted the shelves in the greenhouse showroom in years. Probably nobody had. Why bother? Customers didn't pause here. They went right to the glass houses and the arrays of flowering plants. The greenhouse showroom was always fighting a losing battle against becoming a storage area for overstock and a permanent resting place for dust-collecting cut-leaf philodendrons that never sold and never died. It sank into its half-light of dust, boxes of Christmas lights crammed in the corner during the spring planting season, stacks of Easter-bunny ceramic bowls crowded out of the way behind elephantine potted plants at Christmas.

The downtown store showroom transcended this squalor. It was a stage set for the good life. The design area, where the cut-flower arrangements and corsages were made, was consigned to the basement near the garage as if to hide all evidence of effort. The business office was sequestered in a back warren like a shameful secret. Nothing—not the heaps of stems stripped of leaves tossed carelessly on the floor by the designers, not the careful filing of pale green charge slips by the somnolent office staff, none of it—was allowed to intrude on the front showroom's tableau of luxury. It was an alternative, wonderfully unnecessary world, this sphere where my father spent his afternoons (mornings were for the greenhouse). Here he lavished his art, making the world over as it ought to be for people who, like him, loved loveliness.

A candy shop ran along one side of the showroom, a display case filled with chocolates, caramels, and after-dinner mints in communion-wafer white and sublime pastels (these changed to deep red and a saturated forest green at Christmas). The flower shop sublet this slim space to Mamie Dexter Candies. Like the floral business, Dexter's dated from the nineteenth century, and was still run in the fifties and sixties by Miss Alta, youngest maiden sister of the long-departed Mamie.

Miss Alta was the last of the Dexter candy fortune. Ancient and grim, with the face of Ma Barker, she patrolled her corridor of sweets, a damp cigarette hanging out the side of her mouth. Ashes collected on the shelf-bosom of her black silk dress where they sometimes burned a pinpoint hole. The black silk was shiny as if Miss Alta had been tempered and left to cool into the pudding shape of the chocolates she purveyed to the St. Paul carriage trade. She had a gravel voice and never smiled. And she never gave away samples.

Even my father gave her a wide berth as she plodded from her preserve against the wall to the elevator that led to the basement where her chocolate dippers sat around a wide marble table. These obese women wore white smocks and white hairnets, a bevy of ponderous chemists who appeared to have been dropped on their workbenches like fresh fondant. It was impossible to make friends with them. "Keep away," Miss Alta said in her baleful voice. "They have to concentrate." Two Dexter items, the Uptown and the Mint Sandie, were presented as shop exclusives so she had a point. A missionary in South Africa had a standing order for five pounds of Mint Sandies every Christmas.

The smell of roses and chocolate had a narcotic effect when you entered from Fifth Street. The specialty stores that clustered on the block formed a retail ghetto of extravagance. This wasn't where people like us shopped. But flowers and candy spoke of children and simple pleasures, and somehow made the flower shop all the more tempting, unlike Bullard's, which was formidable to the point of threat, and snobby Frank Murphy with its couture coldness. Gordon Parks had his first job at Frank Murphy, my father said, photographing models for the formidable blue-haired Mrs. Murphy, arbiter of taste who traveled to New York and had known—was it possible?—Coco Chanel. Or had known someone who knew Coco Chanel very, very well. She obtained made-to-order Lilly Daché hats for some of the stylish St. Paul matrons who bought their flowers from my father.

Aside from the public library, the downtown store and the little shops around it were the only Elsewhere of my disloyal, let-me-out-of-here Midwestern girlhood. They promised a Beyond. The flower shop was *here* and it was my father's domain, but it was also marvelously other, this place heavy with the drowsy scent of velvet-petaled roses and Provençal freesias in the middle of winter, the damp-earth spring fragrance of just-watered azaleas and cyclamen all mixed up with the headachy smell of bitter chocolate. Waterford vases winked from glass shelves and broke light into rainbows in the late-fall afternoons while I waited, after a dentist appointment, for the shops of Fifth Street to close for the evening and my father to drive us home, asking me what I learned that day in school.

One night, waiting for him to turn off the display lights, I stood by the big window, and looked idly across the street to Bullard's. The tiny door at the back of the Bullard's display case opened, as if automatically, and a hand, seemingly detached, reached into the little box. It clawed up the diamond-and-sapphire necklace lying on the satin. The door snapped shut behind the withdrawn hand, and the starry strand receded into the fathoms of Bullard's darkness for another lonely night.

A spotlight dazzled the empty display window. A strange bitterness stung me as if I had been denied something essential. Not diamonds and not sapphires. The vacancy of the window was what hurt, oddly. Here was our cold and tidy town, here the narrow window displaying our self-satisfied abdication from all that glittered, here our vacancy that Bullard's illuminated every night. And my father, coming to collect me, with his usual question: *So what did you learn today?*

CHRISTMAS, AT LEAST, made up for every drear St. Paul habit. The downtown store was decked with Noble fir garlands done up with massive velvet bows, the edges stiffened on the back with thin wires to keep the ribbons from drooping. The walls were banked with Fraser firs, the only Christmas tree to have in my father's view, though he had to accept the inexplicable preference for long-needled Norway pines that many of his otherwise tractable customers swore by.

The best Christmas "item" was the collection of hand-carved German and Italian crèche scenes my father bought at the Chicago spring trade show. These Nativity sets were his stealth campaign against the bottom-line thinking of the store's owner. "Who's gonna buy that Italian manger, Stan? You have to mark it up triple with the tariff. You could maybe sell that downtown Minneapolis, but..."

The owner's downtown was not the stuff of my aunt's transcendent metaphor but the small-minded marketplace of the provincial capital. Don't start getting Minneapolis ideas in a

St. Paul kind of town. There was also the problem of theft—
people could nab a baby Jesus in nothing flat and be out the
door before anyone noticed.

My father, I understood, was on the side of beauty, obviously the only side to be on. His loyalty was to workmanship—another word for art. "A lot of people can't tell the
difference in this German crèche," he would say holding up
a well-turned camel sporting a saddle blanket painted in royal
blue and finished in gold scrollwork scattered with minute
gold stars and crescent moons, bearing all the mysterious
East on its back. "But *I* can tell. You put it out there, they'll
begin to see the difference from the plastic. Over time." He
had resilient faith in the educative powers of *just looking,* as
the dopey springer spaniel Buddy and I learned when he took
us for car rides. He was determined to "bring people *up.*"

My mother felt compelled to point out that certain people
saw the difference between the imported crèches and the plastic sets all too well. "Admit it," she said. "Once they've lifted the
baby Jesus, how do you expect that set to sell?" He shrugged.
But later, as Leo the Lion predicted, he had to mark down the
childless manger scenes for the after-Christmas sale, and sell
the pieces separately, like spare parts.

"I tell Ollie and Mrs. Butler," he said, naming the two
widows who were the downtown store's main clerks, "I tell
them to watch those sets. But it gets busy. People can be
quick, if they want to be." He denied the possibility of evil
afoot until the evidence was in, and then he still couldn't

quite bring himself to blame anyone, and saw the disappearance of the best pieces as bum luck. And you really couldn't
get away from that, so what could a guy do?

Being on the side of beauty put you at this sort of disad-
vantage, but once having pledged your allegiance, there was
no going back—or perhaps there was no going forward. Because the forces of modernity were part of the problem. Beauty
had existed from the dawn of human marking and making.
Beauty wasn't simply loveliness for my father. It was the high-
est token of reality. But now this confirmation of reality was
being *chipped away*, little by little, by the forces of mass pro-
duction and plastic.

Modern art didn't help either, splashing paint around,
nothing looking like anything in particular, confusing people,
not bringing them *up* at all—though he admitted there was
some kind of *idea* at work there, though damned if he could
figure it out. Plastic was the real culprit, plastic as a proliferating form of mischief, an almost sentient force, nicking away
not only at beauty but at workmanship and craft that had
been the immemorial proof that beauty was the essential
business of the human world.

There was nothing a guy could do. You could only
keep putting the better things in front of people. And hope
they'd *see*.

LEO THE LION SETTLED into her job at a college library, glo-
rying in her proximity to books. "You really ought to think of

library science," she kept saying whenever I made my claim about wanting to be a writer. In spite of their mutual reverence for education that amounted to a cult (my father was asking me what I had learned today long after I was out of graduate school), working holidays at the flower shop, they agreed, was a Good Thing.

It would not be a Good Thing to be a waitress, nor would my father allow me to take typing in high school. These activities could lead to unfortunate results—rudeness and fanny-pinching (waitressing) or "a desk job" (typing). For typing was the road to office servitude for unfortunate girls without fathers watchful enough to direct them to a real education that in turn would lead to a non-desk job, though he was vague about what non-desk job he had in mind.

"He doesn't want you to end up a file clerk in an office," my mother said. "Like me."

During school breaks and summer vacations my brother was assigned to work with the growers at the greenhouse or on the delivery routes. My father expected me to know the names of plants and to get a sense of the horticultural side of things, but it was understood I was meant for the downtown store, "in retail" where the clerks dressed in gowns they bought on fantastic markdowns from tips passed them by their clerk pals at Frank Murphy and Field-Schlick.

Doctors and lawyers from nearby offices came into the showroom on their lunch hour to order flowers for their wives. Usually their wives. A dozen long-stemmed American

Beauties, off-season, in a box with a card in a sealed envelope, paid for in cash, delivery to some apartment on Randolph, not the man's Lincoln Avenue address—you figure it out.

"Never ask if they want to put it on their charge," Ollie told me. "Sometimes they'll want to pay cash. Never ask why it's going where it's going." She put a well-manicured finger to her lips, the silent gesture of complicity, initiating me into the conspiracy of love now that I was old enough to work at the downtown store. This sort of duplicity was not a green-house thing. The illicit ways of desire belonged to the world of surface and illusion. It proved that the beautiful big room full of exotic flowers and expensive candy was, as my fearful, stay-at-home aunt said, just like downtown.

THE WORK WAS HARD, I suppose, on our feet all day, running around, lifting heavy plants, contending with the prima donna tendencies of the customers. But the place had such drama during the holiday rush when I worked there that the sheer pace of the day, filled with the customers' demanding sub-plots, made me happy—more than happy. I felt important. Or I felt I was doing something important. Which came to the same thing.

A demand for violets might come in. "Violets! Is that woman nuts?" Mrs. Butler would say. But then she would somehow suss out violets from a supplier in Minneapolis by way of Chicago or New York, reaching by degrees all the way to an Amsterdam clearing house with a Parma connection, so that, finally, little drenched purple bundles tied with foreign twine, costing a fortune, made someone on Kenwood Parkway happy.

People came in from the cold, stamping their snowy feet vehemently on the carpet. They rushed up to the marble tables where the clerks awaited as at a battement. Some customers came in looking wild-eyed, holding out their shopping lists like desperate ransom notes. *Can you get a poinsettia to Butte by tomorrow?*

We could. We could send flowers and candy just about anywhere you wanted. We had it in our power.

Ollie and Mrs. Butler, elderly but slim and elegant, worked with the self-possession of head nurses in a triage unit. At the end of the day Ollie took the sheaf of telegraph delivery orders and made her calls, speaking low into the receiver of the telephone by her order desk. *Los Angeles? This is an FTD order from St. Paul...*

The Great World was so far away, but Ollie spoke nonchalantly every afternoon to the coasts. *Let me spell that for you... And would you kindly repeat for verification? Yes, that's Love L-o-v-e comma Bobby B-o-b-b-y. Yes, "y" as in yardstick. No, he doesn't spell it that way. Just the "y."*

You couldn't make any sense out of the ones in Alabama or Georgia, places like that, she would say off the line, they talk so funny. The occasional orders to Europe were sent in the dead of night by telegraph, which was too bad, Mrs. Butler said. If we called them in ourselves, she said, they'd let me try my French... *Paree? Ici St. Paul*...

Like Ollie and Mrs. Butler, I came to respect the customers who knew what they wanted, the doctors and lawyers and their worldly wives who had accounts, for whom buying flowers was a regular part of life. Spenders.

People with taste, Ollie said. She had no time for the once-a-year poinsettia buyers who fussed around, wanting you to pick *the very best one*. She tended them with frozen rectitude, barely polite. Mrs. Butler, though also favoring those "with distinction," had a soft spot for a shy person who came in blinking at the orchids, clutching a ten.

But how could you not admire the people who *knew*, who had poise and a bead on what was what? They were our people. The showroom was for them. The greenhouse had the purity and frank dirt of a farm, but the downtown store was awash in illusion. It belonged to the winners and takers who lived in a zone of carelessness that won our admiration. The best customers often picked up a fistful of trimmed azaleas from the display tables and brought them to the marble delivery tables like employees themselves. As if they owned the place. "Send these off to the people on my list, will you, Mrs. B?"

"How would you like them signed, Dr. Dailey?"

"Oh, Merry Christmas is fine. You can sign for me. Love on the one to my wife."

Dr. Rea came bounding in from the Lowry Medical Arts building, humming an aria (big opera buff, had tickets for every performance of the Metropolitan Opera when it came on tour in May). He bellowed for Ollie as he approached the marble table. "Can you round up a herd of poinsettias? Send to everybody I sent to last year. They're all still alive, aren't they, Ollie?"

They would laugh, Ollie and her best customer. They would agree that everybody was still alive.

He handed her a square envelope with a little bulge meaning a couple of bills were folded inside, a Christmas tip. Ollie and Mrs. Butler never opened these envelopes at the store, never spoke of them though Mrs. Butler once said, "They help." My father was ashamed of what the owners paid them. The office staff, he said, was even worse. "I don't know how Justine manages to eat."

"How do *we* manage?" my mother said, looking up from her book, always ready with a drop of acid. My father shrugged his shrug. "That *company*," my mother said, dumping it as usual into the dustbin of her disdain.

The floor staff and the office staff had worked there for decades. They all lived in apartments, widows and "single ladies" who made up the workforce at the downtown store. There wasn't a married woman in the bunch except for gossipy Rosette who worked the PBX machine and whose husband ground lenses around the corner at Williams Optical. She retired early with arthritis. Served her right. She flirted with my father and I was glad to see her go. All of them took the bus to work, and had two weeks' vacation, which they spent at home "getting caught up," as Mrs. Butler put it. No one went anywhere.

Alone among them, stylish Ollie somehow contrived to take her lunch (cup of soup, egg salad on white, trim the crusts, please) at Moudry's counter across from Frank Murphy where, after lunch, she cruised daily for any couture crumbs that might have dropped to a sale table. Everyone else brought a sandwich from home and ate in the basement lunchroom by the design room near the candy dippers where a game of cribbage was always on. Even Ollie brought a thermos. "Coffee adds up," they reminded newcomers hired for the holiday rush who would squander a good part of an hour's wage, morning and afternoon break, on burnt coffee from Moudry's.

BUT LET'S GET SPECIFIC. The history of innocence would be incomplete without this moment. Christmas Eve, the final mad dash of the holiday and we could count on some of our favorites showing up. These were men racing in from a quick stop at Frank Murphy, carrying shiny black boxes with big pink bows, the Murphy insignia. Ours was the silky powder-pink box with the firm's name cast across it in gold script like a line from the Declaration of Independence.

These last customers of the holiday were classicists, men who bought cashmere cardigans at Frank Murphy and roses and chocolates from us. They came slouching in with their camel-hair coats open. They could leave their shopping to the last minute because their wives had already bought everything for the holiday. All these husbands had to do was make a lavish gesture for the wives. We awaited them at the big marble clerks' table with our pale green order books and our utter exhaustion. Latecomers. They were the easy ones. They'd take anything.

And in he walked, fifteen minutes before closing, an officer of the navy, shoulders squared, a commanding face already slightly impatient. I'd never seen him before. Being in uniform he was certainly from out of town, but he headed straight for our table as if he knew his way around, a man with a mission. My kind of customer. I dipped past the table and made for him before anyone else could claim him.

I didn't often get a chance like this. The clerks didn't work on commission, but none of the big customers, the happy spenders, came to me. If Ollie and Mrs. Butler were busy, their good customers waited for them, wandering around, idly turning over Hummel figurines to check the prices, inspecting the candy counter, putting their faces down to a gardenia's matte petals. Then Ollie or Mrs. B would race over, apologizing for the wait. Sometimes, if a regular customer was in a hurry, he might turn to me standing at the table in my blue-and-white serge convent school uniform, and say, not bothering to disguise his disappointment, "I suppose you could take care of this."

But for the most part I spent my time with the one-poinsettia, cash-and-carry crowd who streamed anonymously in and out during the holiday. My father had told me to "treat everyone the same." He knew the arch manner of Ollie and Mrs. Butler and he didn't try to change them. Maybe he didn't want to: the graciously run households of Crocus Hill and Summit Avenue were our essential clientele.

I adopted Ollie's hauteur, taking a mean-spirited satisfaction in grabbing the first plant I saw on the floor when the low-end amateurs wheedled around, asking me to pick out *the very best one.* In the lunchroom at coffee break we disposed of this entreaty with withering contempt—*Mrs. B, would you be sure to pick out the very best doughnut for me over there in the box Vick brought in?* And Mrs. Butler would pantomime an exaggerated inspection of the doughnuts in the half-sheet bakery box on the sink counter. She paused, shook her head, gazed intently, an expert's discerning frown on her brow as her hand dipped and rose, dipped and rose over the glazed zeroes before her until finally, finally—"Ah, here it is!" she cried, lifting *the very best one* aloft.

No such fool, this navy officer who strode toward me now. I could see that. He was handsome, in a craggy, can-hold-his-alcohol way, modern somehow, not a man with the smooth matinee-idol looks of my earnest father. He'd been around, you felt, had seen the world. Been marked. It was part of the handsomeness. He came forward resolutely, a man with better things to do with his time, ready to hand over his gift list, ready to trust me with the details.

I approached him without my order pad—Ollie and Mrs. Butler greeted their good customers like friends for whom a purchase was somehow a given and yet also secondary.

"How may I help you?" Another Ollie touch—don't say *May I help you?* Claim the next step—*How* may I help you?

"I'm looking for a lot of roses," he said.

I didn't blink. "Red?" I asked professionally.

He looked at me—took me in for the first time I think—as if I might be a tricky one. But this passed instantly. He smiled, a surprise and a charm, that radiant smile coming from that stern face. "Yes," he said, right into my eyes, "Red. For Christmas." We had a small laugh over this meeting of minds—at this season what other color could a rose possibly be?

I led him to the display cooler which wasn't the real cooler (that was in the basement), but the one meant to tempt people with possibilities. Slim pickings. Long-stemmed red roses stood upright, as if at attention, two dozen in a galvanized metal bucket. There wasn't much else left in the cooler, a few buckets of lemon leaf and winter greens, holly and cedar, and several branches of chartreuse cymbidium orchids slashed at the throat with maroon that would require the rare customer with daring taste.

"Those," he said, pointing to the roses with the resolve I expected of him.

Then he surprised me again. "Do you have any more?" he asked.

I could look downstairs.

"Do that," he said.

But downstairs the designers wouldn't let me touch what was left in the big walk-in cooler. *There's still funerals to think of,* they said with the annoyance of people who have to remain at their posts no matter what crazy illusion the rest of the world is off to. Christmas or no Christmas, you had to keep some stock back for death, our bread and butter. *And you can forget about the greenhouse,* they said as I went to the telephone. *They've been out since yesterday.*

"Then I'll take the orchids too," the officer said when I went back upstairs. He checked his watch and looked toward the door. I told him it would only take a little longer while I wrote up the orders. While I was downstairs he'd picked out two vases, a big Waterford for the roses, a narrow one for the orchids.

He wanted everything sent to an address on Bayard, two separate packages, same name on each one, a woman's. I had to tell him there would be a delivery charge because it was so late. He shrugged—fine.

I knew he wouldn't care.

But he was just getting started. A Noble fir wreath and a *tree,* for heaven's sake, to the same address. I had to call the greenhouse about the tree. I explained to Charlie it was for an officer in the navy who had just come home and was shopping late. Charlie, weary but willing, said he guessed so. I can hear his tired voice saying, *Just under the wire.*

Then the officer said he also had an FTD order. He fished in his trouser pocket and brought out a crumpled paper. It was a California address, a woman's name he had to spell for me because it was Spanish. An officer in the navy would naturally have someone with a foreign name waiting in a port city—was Fresno on the coast? Again, he wanted roses, three dozen if possible, loose in a box, no "arrangement." I understood perfectly. Arrangements were somehow domestic, but the instruction "loose in a box" was romantic and—I didn't have this word at the time—erotic. People sent arrangements on Mother's Day. They sent roses "loose in a box" on Valentine's.

And the enclosure cards?

Sign them all *Tom. Love* on everything.

We stood together by the big marble table while I wrote out the orders. As I copied the addresses from the order forms to the delivery slips, I asked him, out of politeness, what his rank was. He was checking his watch and looked up sharply. He didn't answer right away.

"In the navy," I said, confused. Maybe "rank" was the word in the army. Maybe the navy had a different word. Maybe it was impolite to inquire.

"Oh," he said. "Captain."

"Nice to be home for Christmas," I offered, "on leave." The lavish spenders liked to make small talk.

Yes, he said, great to be home on leave.

I asked where his ship was. At this he didn't pause. San Diego, he said. San Diego. He said it twice. Then, "I'm kind of in a rush." He was sorry to have to rush me, he said, but he had people waiting for him. He looked toward the door again. "The holiday, you know," he said smiling. That wonderful smile. The holidays are crazy, I said. We smiled into each other's faces, almost friends.

And how would you like to pay?

He gave the usual formula. "Put it on our account," he said. "You have the address right there," he pointed helpfully, reaching over to the local delivery slips, grazing my hand with his own. "Mrs. Thomas," he said, pointing to the last name, and the address on Bayard. Ah, the wife. I smiled a sophisticated Ollie smile, thinking of the woman with the Spanish name in Fresno who was getting three dozen roses loose in a box to the wife's two arranged in a vase. Well, the wife was also getting the orchids. And the Waterford vase. Score even.

And if California is out of roses? I asked at the last minute.

Something nice, he said vaguely, the way all the best customers talked, trusting everything to us. He was already headed to the door. People were waiting for him.

I thanked him. I added "sir." This apparently pleased him because halfway to the door, he turned as he pulled on his officer's hat, and gave me a little salute and a final Robert Mitchum smile.

The store was empty, the Dexter candy clerks had shrouded the long glass case, and turned off the display lights. Ollie and Mrs. B were putting on their overshoes at their order desks behind the counter. Ollie called to me to lock the front door.

My navy officer, I saw, had gone across the street to Bullard's. He was peering in the door. He pounded on the glass. But I could see that the Bullard's cream satin windows were already vacant. He wouldn't get in under the wire at Bullard's as he had so luckily with us. Probably he was looking for diamonds—whether for the wife on Bayard or the Spanish woman on the coast, it was impossible to know.

WHAT SURPRISED ME when my father asked me to sit down at his desk in the basement office two weeks later was that I *wasn't* surprised. Not really. Even before he explained, I saw it all.

He was so patently phony, my best customer, so absolutely not an officer in the navy or anything remotely military. The jacket was a joke—it came in sharp focus as my father pointed to the orders on his desk. The cuffs were frayed. The wool of the jacket was pilled, not even quite clean. The man's hair was too long. His blue wool tie strangled his reddish neck in a tight knob. And that salute as he left— ridiculous.

The hat's shiny visor was cracked, gray cardboard showing in the little split. It was a costume, not even a good one. And his shoes? I hadn't looked at his shoes. I stayed with his face. The commanding smile. The Robert Mitchum sexiness.

Why was all this so evident now, why was I so easily hoodwinked at the time? I sat at my father's desk and looked at his face that was really severe, not the mock-sternness of the navy officer broadly playacting a big man.

My father brought out a letter. It was from the man's mother. Or rather it was a letter from a lawyer representing the mother. Her address was the Bayard address where the roses and the chartreuse orchids and the wreath and the Christmas tree had been delivered. The letter included a copy of a public notice the woman had placed in the classifieds of the *St. Paul Pioneer Press* several years earlier notifying anyone who cared to know that she, Mrs. Thomas So-and-so of whatever number on Bayard Avenue, hereby disavowed all responsibility for any debts or encumbrances incurred by her son, Thomas Jr., same last name, No Known Address, under any name or alias he might use from this day forward.

Will she pay? I asked in horror.

"No," my father said, looking down at the orders, "we can't ask her to pay."

The navy officer—I couldn't think of him as anything else—had skipped town, he said.

Fresno, I thought. As for the FTD order for the three dozen roses—"We'll have to eat that, too," my father said, a rare weariness in his voice.

I'd been incredibly stupid. Yet he didn't scold, didn't admonish. There was no punishment, no demand or suggestion that I pay it all back out of my own wages. No sermon. I went upstairs to the showroom chastened, but apparently I wasn't in any trouble. All this would be swept under the rug of invoices and receipts, taken on the winds of remittances and debits that gusted through the business office in the basement. It would all just go away.

But did I understand then or is it only possible now, in the middle of the night of the last day of this life, to see in the great framed panels of memory how my father struggled, how trapped he was as he explained the situation to me? There he is, sitting miserably at his desk with the lavish orders before him. I've been an idiot, naïve, so easily taken in. But he can say none of that. He, the great believer in the teaching moment, can use this experience to teach me nothing.

That was his real misery, not the hundreds of dollars I had given away so easily. I wasn't Ollie or Mrs. Butler, I wasn't an employee who had made a terrible mistake and must be wised up.

I was his girl, the girl he'd brought up to be—to remain always—an innocent, an eternal ingenue without guile or mistrust or even too many useful skills. No waitressing, no typing. Something better and more beautiful was awaiting me. Nothing bad could happen to me there in the store where he presided. I was free to trust everyone, everything. He didn't realize that the trust he bred in me, the trust he demanded, dragged in its communion-white innocence the deep shadow of adulthood where, eventually, I'd have to learn the score like everybody else.

But admit it, I was already well on my way to being an ex-innocent. Worse: I was becoming a phony innocent, a pretend naïf. I'd seen it all, but I knew I wasn't supposed to see it. So I un-saw it. Didn't see the fakery. Didn't see the scam. Saw only the charm and happiness of the moment, the handsome man with the fabulous smile and a desire to give lavish gifts. It was what my father trained up in me, Miss Muffet on my flowery tuffet with a wee book of poesy.

I was never to approach the world with narrowed eyes, never to be the one to get the better of anybody. I won't be a file clerk like Leo the Lion, and I won't sit in a corner nursing Celtic grudges, keeping tabs on people. The romantic photograph—the one propped above the piano where I practiced under their lazy erotic gaze—is only a still shot. In the movie— our actual life—their faces are different, or hers is. And not just because they're older. She learned to level the world with a strangely knowing mistrust, an ice chip of irony on her slouched shoulder.

But my father wants me to stay as she was, caught in the romance of innocence. I'm never to morph from the romantic lead who leans with sweet dependence against him under a cottonwood tree along the Mississippi.

Even as he swept the orders from his desk like a bad poker hand, my father said nothing. I wasn't in trouble, I couldn't be scolded. I was what he wanted me to be, his daughter, a truster in the lovely surface of things, another believer. His girl.

How often he still comes back to me, my navy officer. He appears at odd moments—he's here right now, another snapshot I took without knowing it, his face shining at me on the big screen of the night-black hospital window, winking his Robert Mitchum wink.

He comes out of the cold from Fifth Street on Christmas Eve, striding across the showroom, the last customer of the holiday, my best customer ever. The laughable costume, the lavish smile, his final jaunty salute.

Was that ever his lucky day. I was waiting for him. *How may I help you?* He didn't even need to do much acting. I made him up all on my own.

Chapter 6

"YOU'RE A POET," my father said one day out of the blue. Said thoughtfully, and echoing tonight as if he were still waiting for a response. I'd published two books of poems by then, so this wasn't news. But he said it as if acknowledging an unlikely concept. We were in his car, going to a doctor's appointment.

Tonight as he repeats this remark in the dark by her bedside I understand for the first time—how did I miss this before?—that he wasn't making a statement of fact. He was framing a conundrum. He was wondering how this came to be.

Good question, Dad.

You either believe in ghosts or you don't. The stray fragments of old conversations, the voices of the dead—you're a person they talk to, mumbling in your head, or they don't, the little people who invade the mind-heart or whatever this engine of self is.

I struggled, like any mid-century daughter worth her feminist salt, fighting to the death (which is where we are right now), *not to become my mother*. But still they keep talking, the little people of her Irish mind, insinuating themselves— herself—into the crevices of my supposed self. Even my father seems to have become one of them, murmuring vatic remarks in my inner ear, my down-to-earth Stan making a cameo appearance, becoming a bit of poetry, the way a detail turns into an emblem.

A summer night. He and I were standing on the front porch, one of those wild midsummer Midwestern thunderstorms. We were always drawn to the jags of lightning and the ionized air. Mother and Peter didn't join us. They stayed inside, waited for it to clear. But Dad and I always gravitated to the screen porch in a big summer storm.

Peter, his future as an oral surgeon rising in his broody passion for small, sane moves, sat at the dining-room table, holding a tweezer, poised to attach a decal to the wing of the balsa-wood airplane he was finishing. Mother was in her history book, a wreath of cigarette smoke rising around her. *Parnell is dead, dead*. The lightning flashed madly down the black asphalt of Linwood. Somewhere nearby a tree cracked with a terrible contorted basso screech. "Somebody's going to lose a tree over on St. Clair or Lombard," my father said quietly, not really to me. The air was gorgeous, fresh, completely alive.

His hand rested on my shoulder with its lyric weight. Scary storm, but not scary for us. We're okay over here on

Linwood, a block away, a world away from St. Clair and Lombard, and safe.

HE COULD ACCEPT the notion of my being "a poet" better than my mother's idea that I was "a writer." Poets are innocents, they belong to the ether and the earth. They don't narrow their eyes and tell tales as "writers" do, proving in their mean-spirited way that the earthlings are filled with greed and envy, that the world is a spiral of small-minded gestures. Poets, at least, don't tell tales on other people. They celebrate beauty. They make much of little. Flowers, birds, the names of things are important to them. So being a poet was all right, though hopeless.

There was, even in "tragic" poetry, a note of optimism, of hope, the lyric lilt of meaning and significance. And he was determined to be cheerful all his life. A long faithfulness to seeing the sunny side—from the Czech neighborhood down by Schmidt Brewery where Frankie died that awful death, scalded horribly in a giant vat he was repairing. Someone, not knowing he was in the copper chamber, turned on the boiling water. He lived three weeks. Stan was left, the only brother amid a bevy of sisters. Important to buck everybody up. He was cheerful all the way through his two unbroken marriages—to my mother and to the greenhouse.

Only when we went up north, the two of us sitting for hours in the little boat waiting for a nibble on the glassy lake, only then he wasn't cheerful. He pointed out the Indian burial grounds on the side of the river once. *They leave food there*, he said. *It's their religion.*

But for the most part he was silent, absolutely without affect. Finally let down his guard. I would chatter, ask him things. I got nothing—nothing—back. He just sat there, staring. Natter, natter, natter, my voice doing all the cheerfulness, his voice fallen silent as the midsummer fronds of wild rice made low hissing sounds in the wind. His real being, bleached to virtual absence by sun and water, descended to the soundless fish world where you didn't need to say a thing.

Something about silence, something *of* silence was at the resistant core of poetry. Silence had to do with honesty. Just sit in the boat and stare at the lake's untroubled surface. No opinions, no *judgments*. No Leo the Lion—she almost never went out in the boat. Not just because she preferred to sit reading her book by the diamond-shaped mullioned windows he'd salvaged from the greenhouse. *I have that fine Irish skin*, she would say. She could not bear the sun, and on those rare occasions when she did go for a boat ride (she never "went fishing"), she covered up to her fingertips, and wore a vast mushroom of a hat as broad as her shoulders, a blob of white sunscreen on her pale face under its straw eave.

He went hatless, shirt open to the sun, his dark skin bronzing, never burning. *Your father looks like an Indian.* Said with admiration. A real man. But alone in the boat, he and I, all conversation fell like a lead sinker. What's there to say? What you want with your line in the water is down there somewhere. Don't say a word. Don't do a thing. Wait for a nibble from the danky deep. Something will catch. That's poetry.

Still, sometimes he would come out with something—not when the two of us were alone in the middle of the lake's stillness. There silence was supreme. He chose the confessional of the car for his brief revelations. Not long after he said *You're a poet,* as we drove to yet another doctor's appointment, he said out of nowhere, *Your mother's become quite a handful.*

He was referring to the pretty girl with the high cheekbones barely leaning her wandlike body against his under the cottonwood tree. The same girl who walked into World History at Mechanic Arts High School in 1934 and saw him surrounded by the fast set. The girl with a shy smile and dazzled blue eyes. The girl he allowed, in time, to adore him. Who, unbelievably, had become *quite a handful.*

Strange that their courtship story was always hers—but then, all stories were: *The room was on the second floor. I thought I was late for class. I was running down this long corridor that was dark. There were lockers on both sides. I was out of breath when I opened the door. The room was bright and it hurt my eyes. I saw him right away. He was sitting by the big windows on the far side of the room, sunlight was pouring in and I thought: That's the best-looking boy I ever saw. He was saying something and everybody was laughing.*

His own version of their meeting, laconic latecomer to love, adored brother of his three big sisters, best-looking boy who never wanted for a girl, had none of her atmospheric shimmer: *We were standing in line for graduation, and this girl—I sort of knew her, she was a friend of Charlotte, the girl I was going out with—was standing behind me. "I suppose they're having a party for you at home tonight," I said to her. Just for something to say. But they couldn't give her a party at home she said—her grandmother was dying. "Want to go out, then?" I said. And that was that.*

So how did I "become a writer," vocation approved of by Leo the Lion, wondered over by silent Stan? My brother was the first in the family to go to college. He signed up for the straight and narrow, barely eighteen and on his way to becoming a dentist, as serious as if he too had come up out of the Depression. Just four years later, and I was a different generation: the sixties and watch out, a whole lotta shakin' goin' on.

I started as a music major at the University. My career plan was actually fairly decorous too, if stagier than dentistry: I wanted to crash away on a huge Mason & Hamlin before rapt crowds who leapt to their feet, shouting thunderous approval. Flowers are tossed on the stage. Travel whisks me from hall to hall, continent to continent. I bow in my black velvet with the plunging neckline.

When this future laughed me out of the five-hour practice sessions my freshman year—*legato, legato, Patricia, can't you hear it?*—I found my way to the English Department, haven of dashed hopes, which shared the morose corridors of

Vincent Hall with Mortuary Science. There I settled in. No bowing from the stage in black velvet. But hadn't I chosen the wordy life long ago and just hadn't realized it? Think of those girlhood summers lying like an invalid on the front porch, reading reference-book-heavy nineteenth-century novels so weighty they made my arms ache more than practicing the piano ever did.

It was bliss to discover that my work from now on, apparently, was to read a lot of novels and poems in the upper reaches of Vincent Hall while, somewhere below us, the Mortuary Science undergrads did whatever they had to do. I screwed up my nerve and applied for a job writing articles and reviews for the student newspaper and magazine. I acquired a byline.

My first reviewing assignment was a performance by Rudolf Nureyev. A free ticket and a notebook in my lap. A professional. In my review I allowed that Nureyev's jumps were "quite deft."

I felt pretty deft myself. Not only had I never used the word "deft" before, I'd never before seen a ballet. I brooded a bit that I should have said his jumps were "nimble." But even this proved I must be a writer: Wasn't that the job—worrying about whether to use "deft" or "nimble"? And there I was next morning, name in boldface under the headline, giving his nibs a critical pat on the back. Dance on!

Thus began my double life—girl reporter and cultural know-it-all by day, dutiful St. Paul daughter by night. The

University was my Manhattan, locus of art and romance and lovely trouble, dirt and filth, glamour and blessed foreignness. And St. Paul was . . . well, still St. Paul, the cinder hearth to which my arty Cinderella must scurry back before the stroke of midnight.

I fled in the morning in a carpool with my brother and two of his dentist buddies who discussed suctioning and gummy mixtures for dental impressions as we drove down Summit and dipped along River Road, the Mississippi deep in a crevasse below the bluffs, until we reached the campus. *I'm not walking on the same side of the street with you if you're against the war,* my brother said furiously one morning after one of my lashings of the Johnson Administration.

He walked south to the bombastic new medical complex, I turned north where the arts and humanities crouched in the phony classical buildings hugging the Mall. I stayed on campus as late as I could, working on the magazine with my smart new friends who lived in impressively dumpy apartments and had to report in to no one. I tried to keep the fact that I lived at home a secret, but it was impossible to cover this shameful truth. I still went to Mass on Sundays, another humiliating bit of my bio.

When everyone else was talking about hitting the bars, I was rushing to catch my ride at the dentistry building where my brother introduced me as a peacenik to his lab-coated fellow students who stared at this interplanetary visitor from the humanities.

I gazed back in a louche manner. For the first time in my life, I was an outsider. It felt terrific. A tincture of danger glinted in the dark eyes I inherited from my father and the priest-hating Czech side. Yes, I'm against the war. I'm going out with a guy who turned in his draft card. Women's lib— you bet. Marijuana—sure. Believe in God?— I'm still thinking about that one.

Below his buzzed crew cut, my brother's china-blue Irish eyes looked at me, aghast. I was finally getting somewhere.

DREAMS OF ESCAPE. Plots and ambitions. But think again. Is that where it started, at the University? I was supposed to go to the Catholic girls' college. *It's come to our attention that you've applied to the University*, Sister Mary Helen said. She'd called me into her office at the end of my senior year. *You'll lose your faith over there.*

My heart leapt like a fawn.

I was right after all. What I wanted was *over there*. Not just what I wanted, but what I wanted to ditch. Everything they had worked so hard to give me. How I wanted to unload it— and them too. The parental embrace, the suffocating tentacles of love. When I first heard *Sgt. Pepper's Lonely Hearts Club Band*, the ballad "She's Leaving Home," I gasped. John Lennon had plagiarized my life.

I'm running on empty here, this is an endless night—all these nights have been endless. Her hand, so cool, is not dead, and her voice is still alive, if this strange breathing, deep and rhythmic, can be called her voice. Exhaustion is a high, the sparks of clairvoyance snap and ignite connections you never made before.

I'm glad to have this yellow legal pad, notes I'll use to make something. *Are you working? What's it about?* I'm lucky to be a believer in the little cult of note-taking. Crazy, how lucky you feel holding a dying woman's hand in the dead of the night (great phrase—it's earned its right to be a cliché, too bad it can't be used).

So, pivot the building. Turn away from the Cathedral and the History Center. Face the river. Where the city started, where your father took you to see the floods. This is where life begins, creatures making their way, slithering out of mud into air, moving from water to land, from image to story, the evolution of life. That's where all the poetry started, Dad. Where we went together in springtime.

Just don't go down to the river. My mother was speaking sharply as we headed out the back door, Dad and I, for our Sunday ride in the Ford. She stayed home fixing dinner, roast pork, a brittle-skinned baked chicken, some meal demanding no attention, allowing her to sit and read. We go on adventures.

The Mississippi had surged over the St. Paul levee, achieving, as the papers loved to say, "historic levels." These were the floods that ruined yet again—but this time for the last time—the little houses of the Italian families who for generations had settled on the floodplain, trusting to luck.

It was understood, no doubt by my mother too, that the

levee was exactly where we *would* go, that the river was our only possible destination that day. Her hand-wringing ratified the value of witnessing devastation and ruin. Damage drew us to the river, the illicit festival provided by conflagrations, inundations, whatever depredations come near enough—but not too near—to become "sights." Our mind-numbingly ordinary St. Paul world was now illuminated. It was framed by significance. Not simply ruined, but dignified by disaster. The levee was no longer a blear background. It mattered. Was worth a look. Thrilling because engulfed.

About this time, Sister Mary Louise, gentle piano teacher with bulging misty eyes, had me laboring over a watery Debussy piece—*La Cathédrale engloutie*, the engulfed cathedral. Strange title, as if water were rising over our own Cathedral, supposedly safe on high ground, up the hill. Something about that title wasn't just weird—it was accurate to our life in a way impossible to explain. I *recognized* it, submerged for weeks in the murky piano piece I practiced for my lesson. Poetry and music could grasp an accuracy so intimate, it was beyond what you could *say* to anyone. Buried truth was seized up in metaphors and melody. Engulfed, drowned, suffocating—St. Paul, us. But unspoken, almost unthought.

Only poems and music, it seemed, could express the real things, which were the unsayable things. That was odd—that the unsayable things could be expressed and required expression more than anything *because* they were inexpressible. Music, poems could do this. They went beyond "communication." A spreading comfort rippled from this fact, and something of terror too. Poetry and music weren't "stories," weren't social as fiction was social. They came up behind you, grabbed you, made you part of what they said. It was uncanny and captivating.

In Vincent Hall we read Emily Dickinson's definition of poetry. "If I read a book," she said in a letter, "and it makes my whole body so cold no fire ever can warm me I know *that* is poetry. If I feel physically as if the top of my head were taken off, I know *that* is poetry. These are the only way I know it. Is there any other way?"

You were a poet, she was saying, not just if you wrote a poem but if you could really *read* one—the words of a true poem were that exact, that completely in register with the whole experience of existence, they belonged to the one who responded to them. I understood what an *engulfed cathedral* meant. I had played the notes, I took in the mysterious words. Harboring them in this way, I seemed to have written them. They were mine. That was poetry. And everybody harbored this knowledge. That was why poetry was the most important thing in the world.

My father, sitting next to me, driving the car along the floodwaters, was even more exact. He understood this deluge was different from previous floods. Its ferocity would call down federal mandates and earnest city planners with newly devised safeguards, rules, and regulations. More than an event, this flood would be seen as a condition. It would take an essential part of his hometown geography and erase it. Maybe he drove down to the sodden levee not far from the greenhouse on that vacant, gray Sunday in a private salute to his own domestic past—the immigrant Czech neighborhood not far from the Italians along the river.

Such snug urban enclaves were just then eroding. The children of these tight, tender old neighborhoods were taking to the urban margins, to what, years later, we would call sprawl. Not that he ever left. He stuck with the city. The Italians were departing in this drastically biblical way, flooded out, but the effect was the same, if swifter: the disappearance of his world. The Corps of Engineers had already ruled that the little houses must be cleared away. The humans had to go. No federal or state money for rebuilding. The Italians were shooed to the new suburbs, punished finally for foolishly hugging the side of the river all these years.

Think of the pianos! my mother had cried that morning, looking up from the dismaying front-page pictures of drowned houses, the suddenly Venetian streets where boats with outboard motors idled obediently at submerged stop signs. Women on the levee sang opera music as they hung out the wash, my mother said. *Every house down there had a piano!* As if this cultural refinement should have saved them. From this remark I saw cartoon grand pianos with warped veneers of walnut and spruce, their tops propped up like heavy sails as they bobbed down the swollen river, women warbling arias from the tops of doomed houses.

It was the last neighborhood along our part of the river. For years after that, the rest of my girlhood and beyond, the levee was given over to a scrap-metal yard where smashed and flattened cars lay stacked like cords of firewood for a colossal bonfire that was never lit. From time to time bands of homeless people set up temporary camps along the river-banks in the warm months—and were eventually hounded out. The river became the disdained territory of throwaways, used-up objects, discarded people.

Yet now the city has announced it intends to "do something" with the river. Backhoes mound up a steeper levee: a developer has gained rights to build "housing units," luxury condos in the very place where, that spring Sunday, my father somehow convinced a cop in a patrol car that he had business past the police line and needed to "investigate." He used the word—my mild father—with grave command as if he were in charge here. The cop waved us through.

We drove in, water rising to the Ford's hubcaps. Instinctively, I pulled my feet up from the floorboards, my arms around my raised legs on the gray upholstered seat. My father didn't speak, didn't seem to notice me huddled next to him. We might have been in his little aluminum boat, up north, waiting for a nibble. *Dad...Dad*, I said.

No reply. He drove slowly, so slowly I had the sensation we might be sinking, going down, not forward. Engulfed. He leaned over the steering wheel, staring intently out the wind-shield. The water made soft slipping sounds against the car.

These waves were worrisome, but his face was calm. He did seem to be *investigating*, as he had told the patrolman.

He was framing his pictures, I think. Making his album, in effect writing his poems. What was that dangerous snatching of last pictures on the floodplain but the desperate reach of photographic memory, logging his world as it disappeared? Snapshot by snapshot, still after still.

Once, when I was in college, the highway up to his cabin by the Indian cemetery was barricaded by AIM. The Indians were demonstrating for their hunting rights or maybe against the development of domesticated wild-rice paddies. He couldn't get up to the lake that weekend and was uncharacteristically angry.

I knew nothing about it, but of course I was on the side of protest. Any protest. *They have to fight,* I told him archly from my broad English-major view of things. *They're being forced to give up their culture.*

That's what you do, he said grimly. *I had to give up my culture too.* He spoke with the biting voice of Leo the Lion, her growl of impacted fury. Not a fury I associated with him. But there it was—the white ethnic bitterness smoldering just below the surface of his modest upward mobility. You don't protest, don't complain. But there it is under the amber waves of grain.

He impressed on his dark eyes the devastation that appeared before us that spring Sunday as we slid past images of ruin, which, strangely, were not unbeautiful, no matter how

sad they were, sunk in the muck of that ghostly neighborhood, lost finally in wordlessness. *Engloutie.*

He loved the river, was drawn to it. We trailed along it,
out of town on day trips to hamlets well off any main road,
places that betrayed a tendency toward tatter and resignation.
Bitter coffee and Grain Belt, burgers and fries, catfish breaded
stiff as hardtack, and a pool table in the back — *Put some rosin
on your cue, Patricia.* Smiling at his girl who could call a bank
shot to the corner pocket. And in these places, the faces of
people who smoke, who will always smoke, who are not in a
rush because they are calm but because they are becalmed.
Maybe chronically unemployed.

These were the smallest river towns, the ones that don't
even see themselves as towns, just a bar, maybe a marina off
the main channel, bait shop. Two bars, make that three, Tomb-
stone pizzas they can nuke for you.

The Midwest. The flyover, where even the towns have
fled to the margins, groceries warehoused in Wal-Marts hugging the freeways, the red barns of family farms sagging,
dismantled and sold as "distressed" wood for McMansion
kitchens, the feedlots of agribusiness crouched low to the
prairie ground. Of all the American regions, the Midwest remains the most imaginary, ahistorical but fiercely emblem-
atic. It's Nowheresville. But it's also the Heartland. That
weight again: the innocent middle. Though it isn't innocent.
It's where the American imagination has decided to archive
innocence.

The American story line moves from east to west. To end a book with the protagonist standing at the Pacific's edge is, for an American, to achieve narrative metaphor. Whether transcendence or collapse hardly matters—the edge is not just the end. It's the ending. A point much considered in "Narrative Modes of the American Novel" in Vincent Hall.

But we followed the earlier American experience of arrival, of seeking and finding and taking north to south, the *coureurs de bois* and their Indian guides staking our river. "If things had gone a little differently," Leo the Lion, history buff, liked to say, "you'd be speaking French, kid."

Our little drives along the river were dream trips, my father silent as his fisher-self in a boat. We were islands adrift in a mysterious, largely submerged water land called the Upper Midwest, passing by unreal places with mysterious names known mostly to towboat pilots, landings and sloughs without road access or populations, places erased by the Corps of Engineers or never settled, abandoned now except by the agate type used to inscribe their names on river charts—Winters Landing, Coon Middle Daymark, Ferry Ruby Light, Bad Axe Island, Betsey Slough and Millstone Landing, Canton Chute, Winfield Access, Shady Creek, Point No Point.

The automatic elegy of words that name former islands, the poetry of sandy riverbanks, stands of cottonwood and willow, habitations and landmarks long gone, even from memory. This is where he took me, silent Stan, where stories fell silent

and opinions lapsed into the river muck, and you were just supposed to look. Take it in—the beautiful, disappearing world.

He liked to look across the river, watch Canada geese rising
in formation over the great flyway. He appreciated a muddle
of pastel light and mist across wide water. *Just look at that,* he
would say to me or to Buddy, to anyone with eyes to see.

But that flood-time morning as I sat curled up beside
him, terrified of the rising water, frightened that we might
be swept away with the imaginary pianos and the very real
houses, he was on a mission. He was making sure his world,
though lost, would not disappear. He would *see* it. Like Leo
the Lion, he was *taking things in.* But for him there was no
descriptive dash, no yakety-yak. I was not his audience in the
floating Ford as I was hers at the breakfast table. His sense of
notation was different. You wrote for yourself alone, just to
get it down, not to charm, not to enthrall. Lean over the steering wheel, take your silent pictures, don't respond to the
child's alarmed voice—*Dad...Dad...*

Let the kid be scared witless. Forget her, forget everything. Don't say a thing, don't explain, don't comfort, don't
reach out. For once, ditch your responsibilities.

Give over to the heavy lifting of the real freight of your
soul. Take your pictures. Just for yourself, take them. That's
how everything turns to silence, how history passes through
your heart, how the world reverts to poetry.

Chapter 7

FOR ALL MY GIFT OF GAB, I had my silences too, often infuriated, slamming the door behind them all. I was misunderstood—needless to say. I hated them all, my brother who read my diary and laughed—him especially. Strange, how snappish he and I both were, how inwardly furious. Not angry *about* anything. The fury was like sap rising, trying to get out. You're *my only friend*, I sobbed aloud—speaking to my room with the slanted roof as to a person, a trusted confidant. A sign on the door: LEAVE ME ALONE—THAT MEANS YOU!

Ours wasn't the aggrieved story of the misunderstood or mistreated. We were spoiled with devotion.

Leo the Lion would say, *You're independent as a hog on ice.* So much for my attempts to be alone, to be free. It was all ridiculous. Brooding was better than raging. *You vant to be alone,* she would say—not unsympathetically.

There were many ways to be alone in that small house.

Leo the Lion led the way in this department. She said the Rosary, holding the beads tight in her pocket, a good reason not to be interrupted. She listened to the Twins on 'CCO in the dark, another underdog to grieve over.

But reading was the great escape. I hardly understood I was following her lead, summers, the two of us sitting on the screen porch, each with a book, she in Ireland, I on the English moors.

In winter, skating was even better, the whole body thrown into orbit. Ice-skating was my sport, the only athletic passion of my piano-playing, book-reading, indoor girlhood. A northern pleasure, a cold-weather art form. But more than that: skating was urban. Unlike skiing or ice fishing, skating did not belong to the landscape. It did not partake of the wilderness. Nor did it offer the illusion of being at one with nature, the false claim of touching the wild.

The best skating was frankly domesticated—a rink tended and groomed like a Zen sand garden. A rink's severe rectitude was translated into ice laid down in immaculate arrays of water lofted by a solitary man wielding the gray snake of a fire hose under a city arc lamp. There were no Zambonis tooling around the rink sweeping sprays of water onto a perfect surface. Our rink was kept in glass-flat perfection by a man moving from left to right under the arc lamp alone in slow, tai chi movements, the fan of water falling, forming a fresh membrane of ice every night and again every morning.

The city had public rinks, but our neighborhood rink

was a club you joined. The Olympic, it was called, as if gliding on its flawless surface raised you nearer to the gods. And though it was private, the winter membership fee was so low it seemed everyone could—and did—join the Olympic Skating Club. Something that could not be said of the summer tennis membership that we, at least, could not afford. The orange clay tennis courts of summer with their white-painted lines meant nothing to us. In the fall, I counted the days till the last sinewy tennis players gave up, and the air hardened. Then it was safe to flood it all over and make the summer game go away, the spongy tennis courts sunk beneath our austere ice.

The Olympic—oblong rink and grotty warming house— was owned by one of those benign older men who never succeed in leaving boyhood behind and who manage, from purity of heart and hopeless inability to do anything else, to make a living from the games of childhood. His name was Skip. He sold skates and hot chocolate in the warming house, and kept strict rules, though I can't remember what the rules were. But he had no discipline problem. You didn't mess with Skip. It was Skip's ice.

We lived directly across the street from the rink, and I was able to keep tabs on the status of the ice by turning out the hallway light and standing at the landing window in the dark, spying across as Skip unlocked the warming house for early-morning hockey practice, which ruined the afternoon ice, chopped up by the sticks—I had complained to Skip about this several times. "The boys have to practice," he said. "They got games." Said with the urgency of a man commanding men. My point: it wasn't fair to the figure skaters. That is, the girls. I got nowhere. But it was a first feminist moment.

Around dinnertime, Skip flooded the rink for the big Friday-night crowd. Show night, date night, be-there-or-be-square night. I stood at my post on the landing. My brother called from his room, his voice tight with expectation, "They flooding yet?"

We raced across the street, the first ones on the rink, stepped out and made the virgin blade strokes on the perfect surface, our marks incised on the gray gloss of ice, a pearl-dull mirror keen with a frail layer of just-flooded water. The ice, so new, made a particular sound when you first cut it, and this sound—not a squeak, not a hiss, but a cello note like heavy silk slowly, intentionally ripped—grasped the heart and made you insanely happy to be alive.

There were some adults who skated, but not, thank God, our parents. They stayed away. The ice was our world, and their old black leather long-blade skates stayed on a peg in the garage, evidence that they were no longer in the game. We alone flew through the air with the greatest of ease. They had skated once, but that was long ago, in the same lost age when they stood under the cottonwood by the river, leaning into each other.

Skip had mounted a loudspeaker on the warming-house roof and played music that ricocheted off the brick wall of the sweetshop at the end of the rink, creating a bowl of syrupy pop music—"Lady of Spain," and anything by Perry Como, his favorite. He had a no–Elvis Presley policy. Sometimes he played Rudolf Friml waltzes, which we protested strenuously.

The ice was best early in the evening, my brother surprisingly graceful, skating into the wind, pretending he had a stick in his hands, faking to the left, faking to the right. I skated fast too, taking the whole oval as my orbit, nobody in my way, cutting the ice backward, twirling in a dizzy spin, coming out of the spin in a daredevil loop. My skates sheered the ice, and the fizzy sound of the blades said *solo, solo, solo.*

IT'S LONG GONE, of course, the Olympic. But it would be closed by this time of year anyway. April, the nothing time, between skating and tennis. A perfect time to sit and wait.

All the waiting over these years. The hospital beds, the late nights careening to the ER, logy afternoons in doctors' offices, hauling laundry back and forth from rehab units and care centers. No wonder, even though I've been told *you understand... this is it,* I feel unalarmed. We'll just sit here, the way we always do.

Pneumonia, eye surgeries, broken bones, pneumonia again—and yet again. Her various maladies were punctuated from time to time like the clang of a church bell by Stan's relentless cardiac condition, the only thing wrong with him.

One year she stumbled off a low curb—broken kneecap, hideous pain, surgery, her leg never right after that, walking with a cane she used to jaunty effect. The knee was actually worse than breast cancer—she had that too. Dad and I stood on either side of her bed when she woke. She clawed at her bandaged chest. *They took it, Mary,* he said softly, hand on her shoulder, *they had to take it.* She moaned and fell back asleep. She never looked in my direction, perhaps wasn't aware I was there too.

But, ever the teller of tales, she recast the story into a fond mother-daughter tableau: *And Patricia was right there. She never left my side. She's the one who had to tell me.*

As if I ever told her anything.

So cancer didn't get her. And she didn't stop smoking (*Well, it wasn't lung cancer*). She would have nothing to do with the hospital social worker who wanted her to join a Reach for Recovery support group. *A bunch of one-breasted women? Get that woman out of here.* But then, at home, calling me to help her out of the bath, saying fearfully, "Have you seen it? The...wound?"

"Oh yes," I said airily as I opened the bathroom door. "I saw it in the hospital before you were aware of anything. I'm used to it."

She wasn't the only one who could fake the truth for the desired effect. I'd never seen her without the dressing since the surgery. I looked with inward horror and outer bluff as I helped her from the tub, the great gouge of her chest close-up, curving all the way under her arm. It looked like a quarter of her upper torso had been stripped away. It was one of the old-style mastectomies from the seventies, sheaths of muscle lifted away with the lymph glands and breast tissue, and then—whistle in the dark, hope for the best. For years after that she wore a bra with a spongy prosthesis stuffed in one cup. *Where's my breast? Anybody seen my breast?* Then finally she let that go too, going one-breasted into old age like the Amazon she was.

Sometime after the mastectomy she got serious about travel. She had but one destination, of course. She flew to Shannon with a girlfriend from high school, and later with a Catholic tour group, later still with a woman from church. She added Rome one time too. Only it wasn't "Rome." It was "the Vatican." She even convinced my father to go to Ireland once. *It was okay*, he said. *A lot of time on the bus.*

An experience he didn't care to repeat when she lobbied for a return trip. *I've seen it*, he said. *Patricia, you go.* I asked him if he'd like to go to Prague.

Nope.

Holland to see the tulip market?

Uh-uh.

By this time I'd gone to Czechoslovakia—to his bafflement (*Not much fun over there, is it?*), and to her dismay (*Why don't you go to Ireland? They're the writers*).

Some atavistic sense of duty—*offer it up*—urged me forward. Okay, I told my father, I'll go.

The idea of traveling with her, *being* with her, filled me

with dread. The same adolescent revulsion I'd felt whenever she dared to touch me in high school. Even a pat on the shoulder—Stay away! As if she were leaching out the life force instead of giving it.

But this was duty, perhaps the last duty. I seemed always to be undertaking final moments that turned out to be not final at all, just another two-step in death's wily dance. *You'll never be sorry you're doing this,* people said with unctuous approval when they heard I was going to Ireland with her, offering their own stories of last good deeds done, self-regarding vignettes of sacrifices made, efforts expended for parents no longer on the planet. You'll never be sorry.

They didn't understand that she was never going to die. She was just going to keep almost dying. The illogic of this thought refused to budge from my brain. *I wish I were dead, I wish I were dead,* she'd howled on the sidewalk in front of the flower shop—years ago. But wishing doesn't get you there. She would hang by her fingernails from the ledge of life.

Just like her own aunt Mamie, little bit of a thing who'd been born in a stagecoach going west from Minnesota to Oregon—and of course, being us, had scuttled back again to God's country when there proved to be no gold and no decent farmland in Oregon. Ancient Mamie sat on Mr. Williams in our living room, tapping her foot, saying, *I believe I'll have another piece of the lemon angel pie.* She lived *forever.* When she finally went to "a home," my mother visited her every week even when she no longer recognized anyone, when she probably no longer knew she was a person and not just a bit of lost being curled on a mattress.

My mother would become Aunt Mamie and I would become my mother. It was written. Somewhere.

You seem depressed, a friend said. *How do you see your future?*

I'll take care of my father till he goes. Then my mother. Then my husband. Then I'll go.

Good God, she said. *You should see someone.*

But of course I "saw" no one, "talked" to no one. Kept slogging along. My idea of "dealing with" the situation was to snap at my husband over nothing. Then we got to make up That felt good.

It was precisely because I could not imagine her being dead-and-gone, that two weeks alone with her were such an eternity to contemplate, driving on the wrong side of the road from one boggy B and B to another, sharing a room as she snored the ripping snore of a great beast, not the tiny thing she was, waging her tedious battles against the English, and— this especially—greedily exultant to have me all to herself every single second of every day for two whole weeks in God's green land where she could discuss some refinements she was thinking about for the Archive.

Offer it up—the only thing to do.

And then my complete comeuppance: she was the best travel companion of my life. Easy, thoughtful, absolutely without fuss or fear, a natural with strangers, patient with changes of plan and annoying delays. She could not be disappointed, could not be jostled from her good humor, her quiet happiness.

She urged me not to worry about a thing. *Never worry about money*—never worry about anything, apparently. And she knew the history—all those biographies and histories had been refined into brief narratives she could toss off as we passed a church, went by a marker. She made it all come alive. History, her subject.

Her manner with hotelkeepers was assured and simple. She radiated a gracious and—impossible!—worldly self. People *wanted* to do things for her, offer extras. Waiters and clerks in stores relaxed around her, the way we had settled in with the sophisticated customers at the flower shop, the people who knew what was what. The spenders. Except she wasn't a spender. Sensible about money always, her little cache of traveler's checks covering her needs, shocked at the treats I imposed, the restaurants I chose, the nights at the Cork estate with the two-star restaurant. But holding her own there too. *I believe I'll have the salmon,* smiling, assured.

My daughter's so good to me.

Her minions beamed upon me.

Her trim leatherette suitcase with its Eire stickers from earlier trips, the size 6 petite no-iron blouses and skirts tucked neatly on one side, her cartons of Merit 100 Lites and her toiletry case (brush, comb, toothbrush, Crest, Merle Norman foundation and powder, Revlon lipstick, the bottles of Dilantin and phenobarbital) snug against her pumps. Little notebook, each day's events tallied, a list of addresses for postcards to be sent home.

I told her she was a great traveler, a much better traveler than I.

It's a wonderful life, she said. *Travel.*

I suddenly wished for her, as if it would have had no bearing on me, that she had married a diplomat, had gone here, gone there. Traveled. She was that rare kind of person: at home in the world. How had I missed that? Too busy fleeing her reach, dodging the librarian who was stuffing me into the Archive still alive and kicking.

She wasn't at home at home, wasn't domesticated somehow. *I always liked living in an apartment. Less to think about.* She, not my father, belonged to the Great World. He was the householder, the maker of homemade soup, the urger-on of home improvements. It was she who brought the foreign outlaws, Napoleon and Benito, into the house. She would have managed in Argentina, on the pampas, overseeing the vast herd of rhododendrons. Or anywhere.

We had our regime, big breakfast in the morning (*See what I mean about an Irish breakfast—people say an English breakfast, but it's an Irish breakfast*). Then in the little car (*There is nothing to be afraid of about driving on the left. You just have to watch when you make a turn*), down the pretty roads with their sculptural stone walls I kept remarking on (*I'm glad you appreciate the fences, nothing like that in Prague,*

I bet), maybe choosing a destination (*You should know this monastery*), maybe not (*Let's get lost today*), then lunch somewhere sweet with a view if possible (*You spoil me!*), a meander to the next B and B (*Not another of those estate jobs—I like to stay with the regular people. Just give me a mean poke if I snore*).

Day after day of perfect travel.

I worried about her unsteadiness when we walked in the hummocky greens outside Kilkenny where the owner of the B and B put her in heaven by asking, "Do you want an egg, my dear? They're *my* eggs. I only eat my *own* eggs."

At the sea edge at Cork, even on sidewalks in the towns and finally Dublin, our last stop, I clapped her arm in mine, as if I were wearing her like a falcon on my sleeve. It seemed safest and came to feel natural, as if something were missing if she wasn't right there, a light drag on my right arm.

The highlight of the trip, she said, was *The Book of Kells*. From the start she treated it as our ultimate destination, and saved Trinity College for last. *You understand it's not the Catholic university.* But never mind. She'd visited *The Book of Kells* on all her previous trips. They turn two pages every so often, she said, one to show a page of text, another to display an illuminated page. She figured she had seen twelve pages so far.

It's just a Bible, isn't it? I said. She stopped in her tracks and gave me a withering look. *For an educated person you're not so smart.*

Once we were in the museum-dark room, a sanctuary,

she broke away from me and bustled up to the glass vitrine, fending her way through a tangle of people with her cane. She looked around impatiently for me. *Get over here.*

She had opened a space and presented, as if it were her own, the jeweled book. "This is the beginning of literature," she said. Where she got this idea wasn't clear, but the triumphant look on her face made it impossible to question. "This you had to see. People *died* to preserve this book."

And then, daily dessert hound, she wanted tea and cake.

We flew home from Shannon. Nothing bad had happened—I couldn't believe it. Better than that. Ireland had been a revelation. *She* had been a revelation. I realized, dumbfounded, the last time I actually paid attention to her was when we were in the kitchen together, she smoking and unfurling her descriptions of the charity ball of the night before, I imagining my way into the scene. *Can't you just see it, darling?*

The rest had been feinting and lunging, the daughterly duel of distance. In fact, had any of us listened to her? Nights at the dinner table, Dad asking what we had learned, but everyone cutting in on top of anything Mother said. One dinner, in the silence of just eating, she suddenly said in an arch dinner-party voice, "Well, Mary, what a lovely meal. You made it yourself?"

"Yes, I did," she replied staring at us with frigid courtesy. "Yes, I did, and I'm so glad someone is enjoying it. So *good* of you to say something."

No one laughed. And no one replied. She was left to talk her airy nothings to herself.

We walked off the plane together, arm in arm, each of us holding a small carry-on bag. At the end of the jetway stood our men, each with a bouquet, smiling in the light. I dropped her arm, the first time I'd done that in days, and ran to my husband, let my little bag fall to the ground and threw my arms around him. Dad stood to the side waiting for Mother who came tottering along, as joyous as I, rushing toward him.

Then, half blind from the bungled cataract operation and blinking in the light, she tripped over my bag, and fell to the ground. And broke her knee all over again.

She left the airport in an ambulance.

My father turned on me in helpless fury. *Why did you let go of her? It's all your fault. You can't let go of her.*

Chapter 8

ONCE HE WAS ABLE TO afford them, my father bought Buicks, big Dad-cars. A Honda, a Toyota, a VW? Foreign cars weren't on his map, and he seemed never to have coveted a Cadillac, but he was gratified to leave behind the middling world of the Ford and Chevy, the cars of my girlhood. He bought his Buicks from the same dealership on University Avenue where he bought the forest-green trucks for the greenhouse. He believed he was a valued customer, he who valued his own customers. He believed they gave him a deal on his own car because he bought the company trucks there. It was the sort of thing he believed, without any particular evidence but with certainty. Good faith was repaid. A firm handshake, a sincere smile. He practiced these things.

On the day I'm thinking of—often think of now, especially tonight when he's come to be with me by her bedside as if we were sitting together in the boat, waiting for a nibble on

Lake Minnewashta—I was driving the next-to-last Buick. Each Buick seemed bigger than the one before, though this wasn't the case. He just kept getting smaller. He stood straight as he always had, upright as a military man, which he never was. But he was shrinking. Still handsome, more elegant even than during his gleaming Valentino years. A refined husk of his earlier self, an inviting calm on his still-unlined face.

It was late May, the lilacs were rusting. I was driving the Buick because, without discussing it, that was how it had come to be: I did the driving, taking him to his weekly appointments with his cardiologist who micromanaged his congestive heart disease like a junk-bond trader, moving the numbers, dumping and acquiring meds in a frantic shell game, always playing the edge. The first heart attack came in his fifties, soon after he made the romantic leap and bought the flower company from the last family owners who were only too glad to unload it.

After that there were two open-heart surgeries, then a pacemaker installed like an internal military medal high on his chest, followed by episodes of fluid on the heart, breathlessness—the works. But still pumping. Past eighty and still going to the greenhouse to play 500 on coffee break, still doing his oil paintings, even keeping up the violin, scratching away for hours till he got Dvorak's *Humoresque* pretty well wrestled down to the mat. It seemed that between his heart attacks and my mother's various maladies, much of the nation's upward-spiraling cost of health care could be located.

We pulled out of the driveway of the condo building over-looking the Mississippi where he and my mother had moved only six months earlier. They lived forty-nine years in the bungalow on Linwood they called 1071 as if the number were a Christian name: 1071 was the house they meant when they said "home." When they spoke of returning to where they lived, they didn't say they were going home. They said "back to the condo."

Mother was in the hospital, tubes everywhere. She'd had a terrible seizure, what looked like a *strenuous* seizure, her stick arms thrust out like rods from her churning body and grim, clenched face. "Leave her alone, let her stay in bed. She'll never be right," my father said, turning away. All this after a stroke only five months earlier, just after they had moved into the condo. To everyone's amazement, Leo the Lion fought back from the stroke. She was home three months—and then the seizure hit her, a vicious aftershock, worse than the original earthquake of the stroke.

This seizure, we felt sure, was the end. It was more damaging than the stroke. But on the morning we were driving to his doctor's appointment we had just been told that, unbelievably, she was going to make it again. Time in a "care center," another round of physical therapy. Trach tube out, breathing on her own. Feeding tube still in, but out pretty soon, and she'd be eating on her own, gloppy messes and slugs of Ensure. A course of occupational therapy that we'd learned had nothing to do with job training; it was about trying to keep dementia at bay. But she'll come home. Eventually.

Heart attacks for him, brain attacks for her. It wasn't clear who was going to reach the finish line first. For a while she had seemed to pull ahead of him.

On that soft May morning, on the way to the doctor, he sat patiently, buoyed up by the Buick's pillowy leather seat. He seemed to have lost his old habit of spasmodically depressing an imaginary brake pedal when I was driving. He just sat, looked out the window at the spring green.

He had his pills—many little root-beer-colored plastic containers—in a ziplock baggie. The doctor would look at them, copy dosages onto his chart, a document now inches thick, limp and frayed at the edges like a sacred text much thumbed. "I still have some tricks up my sleeve, Stan," he said last time, working his numbers, writing new scripts to take to Bober's Drug on Grand. He would say something like that again.

My father would probably ask once again, as if it were a matter of no personal interest, just a disinterested inquiry, if it might be possible to do anything about the itching. Last time the doctor shook his head, mentioned his wife's terrible itching during a troubled pregnancy, how he could do nothing for that either. Stressed kidneys, he said. "Did she get over it?" my father asked, raising his slightly yellowed eyes to the doctor's face for the first time with interest. Oh yes, the doctor said. My father nodded, faint ghost of a smile as his head lowered again.

Impossible to tell what he did with this information, whether he took it as potential good news for his situation or counted himself out, given the pregnancy aspect of the other case. "We're all so impressed with your father," the doctor had told me. "He bears his suffering without complaint. Always a smile for everyone. A real gentleman." This unaccountably annoyed me.

Whereas my supposedly invalid mother, in the hospital, has kicked an attendant in the backside. "Get away from me, you fatty!" she screamed from her wheelchair. I ran around doing damage control, the florist's daughter bringing in long-stemmed roses to mollify the offended party who looked neutrally at the flowers and said, "You don't have to do this. We're used to it." But underneath my groveling, I'm not dismayed. Kicking makes sense. It's my father's gentle smile, the absence of complaint that grind my heart.

In addition to the baggie full of his meds, he holds a small bundle of envelopes bound with a rubber band, all stamped, ready for the mailbox. Bills he will have paid on the dot, the Stan-and-Mary way. He has taken over that task, as he has taken over grocery shopping, cooking, and just about everything else. My mother does almost nothing.

She sits, she stews.

She smokes.

Mother, don't you think all this smoke is bad for Dad's heart? I mean with the house closed up in winter?

Oh, piffle.

She pretends to read, but reading is now almost beyond her. She's more than half blind (the botched cataract operation) and though we don't say it, there is brain damage. Just as we never said she had epilepsy. When I come upon her, sitting on Napoleon, sitting in profile like a blind person (well, she is a blind person really—another thing we pretend is not so), she strikes a pose like Whistler's mother, only not serene, not a peaceful granny. Ours was never a family given to talk therapy, to the comforts, whatever they are, of "talking things out." She got precious little sympathy as she lost one power after another.

A small printed return-address label is fixed to the upper-left corner of the top envelope in the little stack of paid bills my father holds. I glance over to see if he's remembered to order new labels with the condo address. Yes, there's the new address. But the first line of the label reads "Stan R. Hampl." No Mr. and Mrs. No Stan R. and Mary T.

Mary T. is gone.

Idly, I mention this—*You forgot to put Mother's name on the address label*—pointing to the envelopes in his hand. He flushes, a guilty husband found out. "Well, I didn't think she'd...you know...I thought I'd be, you know...on my own." His hand presses into the stack of envelopes, squeezing them out of nervousness, the way he used to press his foot on his secret brake when I was driving.

I've caught him, and I'm sorry. Of course he was hoping to be *on his own*. Released finally, and not by his own death.

That's when he spills the beans: *Your mother's quite a handful*. He's baffled. *She was so sweet,* he says, *she used to want to do everything I wanted to do*.

I keep my gaze trained straight ahead. Our faces are in profile. He isn't really speaking to me anyway. He's in the confessional of the Buick, the secure box where he can murmur his sin of exasperation, of exhaustion. The trademark Stan-wonder fills his dismayed voice, grieved by the desperate disappointment she represents, the betrayal of his expectations that has kicked him in the heart.

He seemed mystified that her bridal docility has disappeared, lost in whatever acid elixir she sips as she sits, half blind by the window, medicated for decades along every nerve-inch of her tiny body, white wine in hand, cigs at the ready, her magnifying glass poised over yet another volume proving the abused lot of the Irish. All that sweetness gone bitter.

Why had she changed? Why should anything ever change? *Plus ça change, plus c'est la même chose,* his high-school French had taught him to say, a phrase he loved to repeat— didn't that mean that the more everything changes, the more it all stays the same? It's supposed to.

She was so sweet, he repeats, shaking his head slightly, still perplexed by this switcheroo, this assault on his worldview.

She's in the photograph over the piano, I want to tell him. In her jodhpurs, barely insinuating her wandlike body against yours. You're there too, grinning and abashed. She's *back there*. Things do change, Dad. Innocence is a temporary, maybe even an unreal, condition. Destined to die.

Innocence lost is supposed to be experience gained, and therefore not a bad trade. *The fortunate fall*, as Professor Youngblood taught us in Milton 3111. But what if innocence is never lost, never forfeited? Then it can't rise to the edifying abstraction of "experience." Can't become "material"—the way writers tame every gut punch and misery life doles out.

The rare innocence of my father never hardens into experience, into knowing what's what. He never achieves irony, the consolation prize for losing innocence and gaining experience. He remains one of the strenuously innocent. It would be comic except that innocence is never comic when it's an article of faith.

There's more: he expects this innocence of me too, at all ages. Flash on the oil painting of *Patricia's Garden* again. Miss Muffet reading on her tuffet. The beflowered poetess. It's the opposite ambition of my mother's attempt to turn me into the observer, the notetaker, the smart cookie unconvinced of surfaces, unpersuaded by good intentions, preternaturally watchful. The cold-hearted girl writer on the go she can lodge in the Archive.

My father absorbs the betrayal of his illusions not with bitterness but with disbelief. Every time he's "let down" by someone (his mild term for treachery), he doesn't get angry. He turns back, bruised, to the radiant origins of his belief in people and the essential rightness of the world. The great weight of the Cardinal Virtues written in gold around the Cathedral dome is inscribed also in his heart: Fortitude, Tolerance, Prudence, Justice.

He remains cheerful, just as he knew he must be when Frankie, the family hero, lay dying for three weeks in the hospital after he was scalded horribly at the brewery. My father has sustained his quiet cheerfulness, a kind of courtly grace, until he reaches this latest Buick that is conducting him to the man in charge of his dying, who will compliment him on his good attitude.

But here, in the mobile confessional, he's been caught, finally, and by me of all people. Caught harboring a dark and disloyal thought. *I thought I'd be, you know...on my own.*

IT'S NOT TRUE that I found complete solace in the role of the observer, that I reached out for nothing else against the blanket of devotion they tucked around me. Remember that time, one moody season years ago, when I took up my artillery position, trying to sort out what the wise woman I paid by the hour called "my choices." That is, men. *We should also look at your Family of Origin,* she said. Mother, father, older brother. This would shed light on *my choices.*

My parents, already old and unwell, but not yet on the final long lap of their illnesses, came obediently to the little office with the shiny green plants and the Kleenex box on the coffee table. They sat, my father smiling bashfully, my mother glowering. *Why do you go talking to that woman, that stranger? Why don't you come and talk to me?*

My father mentioned the good health of the green plants in the office, an attempt to break the ice with a professional compliment. Mother offered as her conversational gambit her acid silence and dead stare. The therapist, wrapped in nubby earth tones, waited them out with her goddess-calm.

Strange that I have no recollection of what we said, what was asked, why I felt compelled to haul them in there. I see my mother's fury, my father's trustfulness, both of them struggling awkwardly at the end of the hour to fight their way out of the low-set chairs. All that's left to memory is the mixture of my self-righteousness (about what? gone, gone) and guilty misery (occasioned by *my choices* or maybe the Family of Origin) as I watched them struggle to rise in that alien, hygienic room.

What I do remember: after our "session," they left together, down a narrow flight of steps. I was staying behind to "process" the session.

"We thought we'd go across the street to pick up some vacuum cleaner bags," my father said apologetically, as if domestic detail were a betrayal of whatever high-stakes meaning I was after from them.

I watched as they made their way across the busy street, through the parking lot, to the big white building where, two little stick figures arm in arm, they disappeared, as if supplying the answer to their mystery after all, spelling it out for me as they entered beneath the department store's huge logo: POWERS.

Before I imposed that midlife urgency of self-definition on them, ours was a family too earnestly unconscious, too profoundly fixed in the constellation of St. Paul's ethnic and socioeconomic indicators to imagine that "psychology" was a word that might apply to *us*. Therapy was something you sought if your knee went out.

My brother's occasional jags of rage drowned in the flotsam and jetsam of routine. My mother's evenings blurred and slurred when her meds and her white wine fuddled her. Never mentioned. And her vigilant secrecy about her epilepsy (*Never tell anyone. Never!*) meant that the family door was bolted against any mention of mental health, nerves, the very fact of psychology. It was all nonsense anyway.

As for me—I should eat more. I only ate white things— mashed potatoes, glasses of milk. *You'll get blown over in a strong wind.* She stood at the door in the morning with a mug of Campbell's chicken rice soup: *I know you don't like breakfast, but you used to like chicken rice...*

We were pieces of a bigger puzzle. We fit snugly into the design where life had pitched us. Old St. Paul was wrapped in history and money, riveted to the mid-century moment of our mid-continent midsize city, the time-place where my father's decency was a fragile assurance, my mother's growing ferocity and evening befuddlement were a terrible claim, my brother's dark frustrations and my own inchoate ambitions were barely perceptible fissures in the smooth surface.

We glided across the ice rink of family life, trusting we left no gashes as we went round and round the tended circuit of days. We had faith—in everything. Faith was a form of stasis, not transcendence. We didn't live in a movie, the narrative building to climax. We lived in photographs, as nostalgics do, a sweet moment snapped and set on the mantel by the piano where it keeps time at bay, covertly aging in full sight. We believed in love and happiness and small domestic pleasures, duty, and work. Work especially. Work, of course, included school. Education was the height of work.

We didn't talk about ourselves as if we were projects, works under construction. Nobody had a "self." That all started when I went to the University. Only then did it seem that you—you yourself—were detachable from the tableau of family and especially of this family in this city in sublimely static Minnesota, situated at the nosebleed north of the country.

Our life was boring (my point—let me out of here). Or it was beautiful (my father's fervent belief, a man who began the day by humming "Oh, What a Beautiful Morning"). Mother didn't enter into these constructions. Cigarette in hand, she followed the heartbreaker Twins on the radio, read her histories and political biographies that proved to her satisfaction the victim status of the Irish, giving over to a furious sense of the world's essential unfairness.

My brother kept his own counsel, speaking only to his collie on long solitary walks in the leafy neighborhood, as if he were planning his getaway to the West Coast long before he left. Even in winter he and Champ padded along the white streets. You could see his lips moving as he came up the stairs, the dog's narrow head titled toward him, attending closely. Mother, always alert to any aggrieved heart, warded me off. *Don't tease him. He needs to talk to somebody.*

The Upper Midwest, our place, seemed to have transcended the regular Midwest, and our Siberian ascendancy gave us an almost imaginary existence amid the boreal forests of dark winters and silent stars. Ours was pre-freeway St. Paul, a time-place where it was possible to spend an entire lifetime without straying over the Minneapolis line where the Scandinavians went about their Lutheran business. Our social status was unspoken but somehow deeply etched, smack in the blameless middle, looking up without greed and down in solidarity.

And religion? Pre–Vatican II Catholic, what else? Confession in the little boxes on Saturday night before the movies, whispering humdrum sins into the bored ears of Father Kennedy or Father Slattery, avoiding the eternity of Hail Marys doled out by punitive Monsignor Cullinan.

The dual (and dueling) ethnicities of our Czech father and Irish mother were all the psychological typing we had. They divided the world between them. A case in point: The year before they moved from 1071, the bungalow that was home for almost fifty years, a neighbor my mother had her bead on (*drugs over there, I'm telling you*) had come home late and missed his own driveway, plowing into a fence my father had put up to obscure the garbage cans and had faced with flower boxes spilling over with petunias.

The next morning, Dan, their favorite neighbor, an artist with a young family, who had become practically an adopted son, came over to survey the damage with my father. They were deciding how to proceed with the repair. My mother shot out the back door. "Aren't you going to *do* something?" she cried in fury at my father.

The two men looked up at her, mystified. "We're measuring," Dad said. "We'll fix it."

She gave him her withering scowl. "I have to do *everything*," she said, and stormed past him to chew out the drug addict next door. The fence, the petunias—who cared? The point was not to fix what was broken. The point was to take on the forces of evil. Set the miscreants straight. She bustled over and rapped smartly on the door.

My father turned to Dan and said mildly, "I'm Czech. She wants me to be Irish."

The Czechs down by the greenhouse were the world of food and kitchen gardens, a serious interest in prizefights and much music (my grandfather's concertina, giving him vibrant voice, covering his desperate stutter). This was the work hard, play hard Eden of childhood truths and treats. *Run out in the rain*, my Czech grandmother would say urgently, *run quick!* I flew out the back door, naked, screeching with demented joy, to stand under the drainpipe, rainwater sluicing down my tadpole body.

Impossible to imagine such libertine body-delight up the hill in the cabbage-scented halls of my mother's Irish side. There aunts and cousins clustered in rental units within walking distance of one another. They all lived near the monstrous Cathedral. And, as if acknowledging their feudal relation, they were minions of Catholic orthodoxy, and of rule-keeping of all kinds.

The Czech grandmother hated to see me reading—bad for the eyes. Whereas the Irish asked if you had done your homework. They gave books for Christmas and expected not only thanks but book reports in return. They drank skimpy fingers of whiskey, not the rollicking bottles of beer of the Czech side.

Unlike the Czechs, the Irish didn't own their homes. Yet somehow it was understood that my mother had married down. It was the telltale *broken English* of the Czech side that made the difference, as the Irish said either regretfully (the nice ones) or disdainfully (the snobs). But this was overlooked, given my father's handsomeness, legendary and sighed over by several generations. He had inherited his father's stammer, but he made his way around it. And he too had music to cover the language problem—the violin. But polkas and all that knee-slapping? The Irish in their cramped apartments on the ridge by the Cathedral still looked down on the Czech householders drinking beer below the hill.

WE DROVE THE ELM-SHADED streets of St. Paul Sunday mornings after Mass on a busman's holiday to the Como Park Conservatory in the Ford, Mother and Father stationed in the classic leadership positions in the front, Peter and I enacting the turf wars of the backseat. A hermetic feeling pervaded the car, my father taking us on these trips that went, in fact, nowhere, presenting St. Paul as all the destination a person could possibly desire. I curled up in a surly corner of the backseat, a proto-Buddy, refusing to look at "the sights," taking a book along and staring fixedly at it, proving I would travel as far away from the cocoon of ourselves as I could manage. I am windswept on the English moors, leave me alone.

As we approached Como Park, Mother pointed as usual to a spreading forest-green wood house with a gracious wraparound screen porch set back from the street on an even grander lawn on the grounds of the park, the lofty canopies of old elms casting the whole place in shade and solemnity.

This was the sheriff's house, she said. A voice spiked with the Kilkenny acid. The house was the emblem of an abiding family political grief: my Irish grandfather, hotel barber and small-time Democratic Party ward heeler, had backed the wrong man for mayor in a key election, and—worse luck— "lost the position that was promised."

What position? I would ask her when this story came up, as it always did when we drove to Como Park. The words "position" and "promised" shimmered in a sinister way, this life we almost possessed in the shady majesty of the city's oldest park. A sheriff? I saw a horse, a ten-gallon hat, my plump Irish-barber grandfather improbably atop the horse, the cowboy hat atop his head. This was a sheriff. A gun in a holster. It was all unlikely, but vivid, this world we had lost. Just as we had missed the gaucho life and the spotted pony when my father hadn't taken the job at the rhododendron ranch in Argentina. Only this was no choice, no lack of gumption. This was bum luck.

A we-wuz-robbed sensation pervaded the car, drifting from the front passenger seat where my mother sat, the sheriff's dappled estate falling behind us. The house wasn't far from the park conservatory, my father's favorite place. He paid no attention to the sheriff's house or even, probably, to the story of its loss. He always seemed filled with happiness as he took the turn off Lexington, up the rise into the park, where the conservatory's Victorian glass dome rose like a silvery moon filled with palm trees and bromeliads.

But for this twist of unlucky fate, I understood, we would be living in the forest-green house. My father, instead of working just off West Seventh at the greenhouse, would somehow be in charge of the conservatory, the fern room and the palm house, the sunken pool garden that even in winter held a tropical paradise while outside the wind howled across the glazed snowfields of the park's abandoned golf course.

But *the interests* had backed someone else for mayor. *The interests* decided everything. They were murky forces, un-named, mighty in power, extensive in their reach, and Protes-tant. The English again, up to their mischief. My mother believed in *the interests* as her Irish grandmother had be-lieved in *the little people*. But then, my mother believed in the little people too, and in all fierce and conniving forces. The graceful green house set in its shady splendor, this is where our mother would have—I understood *should* have—grown up, not as she actually did in the drab apartment on Marshall where she slept on the living-room sofa till the day she left to be married.

She seemed to accept this lost paradise of the green. This was just politics: doing certain things for a certain party, a per-son with prospects, being promised a position, a grand house that would change your life forever—or not, if through no fault of your own you'd backed the wrong man.

And what things did you need to do to be promised a po-sition? What things had my barber grandfather done?

"Nothing bad," she said vaguely.

What could a barber do? Cut the hair of the man who made the promises? For free? "Grandpa had a chair in the barbershop in the Ryan Hotel downtown. He knew a lot of people." But it didn't matter what you did, who you knew, if you didn't have the luck to back the right man. And, apparently, you only got one chance for that sort of luck.

I sensed that my mother retained the pleasure of proximity to this other life. Or that, simply, she liked the story, liked being lifted out of the everyday into any story. She didn't need the green house itself. She needed the possibility of it—and, even more, she required the loss of it. The loss was precious, an Irish legacy. A confirmation of the perverse, unbiddable nature of the forces running the world behind the delicate scrim of daily life that divided *us* from *them*. The interests. We were innocent of all that.

My barber grandfather's brush with the big time was somehow attached in my mind with his mysterious death. He died before I was born, during the war, and his death was part of how he came to me as a personage, as a character in our family story. I knew him only as a dead man. As I knew Uncle Frankie on the Czech side. The dead were the most important. They made people cry, they made people fall silent.

My Irish grandfather had gone to the hospital for exploratory surgery—there was fear of cancer. It turned out he didn't have cancer. No tumor of any kind. But once the dread word had been uttered—*cancer*—he refused to believe the good news. He was convinced the doctor was lying, refusing to tell him the awful truth. For the truth was bound to be awful. His wife couldn't convince him, nor his two daughters. He refused to get out of bed. Turned his face to the wall, a perfectly healthy man, let his lungs fill up, and died of pneumonia in a week.

The willfulness of it took my breath away. I recognized it. My mother on the sidewalk in front of the downtown flower shop crying, *I wish I were dead, I wish I were dead.* The fury at life for being mortal, painful, unimpeachable in its powers. A person should be able to rise above all this. Or, if not, then die, just die for the spite of it. Years later still, a Jewish friend, after a visit home with me, said, "Your mother's so Irish, she's almost Jewish."

I understood dimly that for the Czechs there were no such choices as those my mother and her father, the Irish pillar, invoked, no such luck, shrewd and canny, no promises either fulfilled or broken, on the Czech side of our life the way the Irish side was ever vexed. No ghosts and ghouls, no dark *interests*. On West Seventh you stayed put. You worked. You were in it together. The imagination was not snagged by forest-green estates, not perversely comforted by bad luck and loss, didn't want to die.

Paradoxically, the Czech world where religion was a cheat—*priests are crooks*—was more faithful than the dream-beset Irish with their accounting sheets of woes. The West Seventh faith was for itself, the huddle of family dinners, weekend fishing, picnics, the closed circuit of the Old World. It was the credo of family happiness: you can look back, but never look beyond.

The Irish lived the dangerous dreams of the imagination, toyed with the notion of rising and falling. And if politics failed them, religion never did—Mother Church with its swirling upward mobility of the spirit, a sturdy hierarchy, both earthly and spiritual that was eternal and infallible.

Not so on the Czech side where even heaven was suspect—those crooked priests—and life was earthbound, riveted to West Seventh realities. Life was not a dream on West Seventh. It was work (the brewery, the greenhouse), it was gardens and groceries (all the cooking and eating in those Mitteleuropa kitchens). And don't forget death, Frankie lying three weeks in Anchor Hospital, knowing there was no hope. "My privates are gone," he said to my father, his kid brother. "It's over."

"He knew," my father said.

Warmth and safety, small pleasures, unspeakable wounds, concertina music, too much food, the talk at the lunch table of what would be served for dinner—this was the ever fulfilled promise of West Seventh. *Nobody had anything.* That was how to be happy. Have nothing.

My Czech grandmother even made a name for herself as housekeeper to "the Justice," Pierce Butler, when he came home from Washington during the Supreme Court's summer recess. They all swooned for her Nothing Soup, so called because it was made from next to nothing. A smear of bacon grease in a cast-iron frying pan, toss in a chopped onion until the sugars burn along the edges, spoonful of flour, water, salt, grind of pepper, parsley from the kitchen garden. The fancy family begged for Nothing Soup as if for elixir. It was their favorite. Proof positive: people up the hill who could have anything longed for what we had—nothing.

THE IRISH SEEMED to die in rank order, old in their beds. And it was the Irish, higher on the hill, who were given to high hopes and intrigue and the score-keeping of religion and politics, the tending of old grudges and grievances. The color of hope was green, the nuns told us in school. And of envy.

The Irish also owned education. That's where the you're-going-to-college absolutism started—with the book-reading Irish. Great-aunt Aggie who had an education degree and had worked for the State of Minnesota inspecting country schools, traveling by sled in the winter, took it upon herself to question even the Church when it came to books. You could do that if you had an education. She let it be known she read books that had been put on the Index. What books? Vague about that, but she was not ashamed to be reading *Doctor Zhivago* as soon as it came out, though it was a known dirty book. *I wanted to see for myself,* she said, and there it was, bold as brass on her night table in the little apartment on Grand. Seeing for yourself was what college did for you. Trafficking in freedom.

She was also, amazingly, a divorcee. Husband came after her with a carving knife, and the priest said she had to divorce him. A priest counseling divorce! Of course she could never marry again. *And don't think there weren't opportunities,* Leo the Lion said knowingly. She broke a heart or two. This was better than love itself, breaking hearts.

The Irish side was soggy with spite—dashed hopes, missed turns, bad bets, rotten deals, deep sighs—given over finally to a swoon known as trust in the good Lord. Bile and treacle, sentimentality and bitter gall. My mother's shudder when she, Minnesota born, would say "the English" as if she were huddled by a smoldering peat fire instead of sitting in an apartment a stone's throw from the monster Cathedral that claimed the city for her kind, the Irish Catholics.

My father, on the other hand, was unable to muster outrage, incapable of grudge. "What did you do?" I asked him on one of our trips to the doctor when I mentioned the time he discovered the original owners of the flower business had been embezzling money right under his nose as their manager. Did I expect him to call the cops, turn them all in, initiate an endless legal ensnarement? Wear a wire? Inform? Did I expect him to quit? Just *walk?*

"I made a fist in my pocket," he said.

But he didn't say it that way. He said, "You make a fist in your pocket."

He spoke not from the first person—what was a self but dust and forgetfulness making its predictable gestures out of deluded self-regard. He spoke from the intermediate second person, from the abyss of powerlessness to which we all are heir, the communion of inevitable suckerdom. He was dislocated from the grandiosity of personality and inner moral assurance. He did what any person—*you*—did when surprised by deception. *Made a fist in your pocket.*

His voice had the mournful discretion of one who honors peace above righteousness, who believes in the calm before and after the storm, not in the storm itself where human bad behavior rages. Realizing that "they were all in on it" was a shock. He admitted that. It cast him, spent, out of the tempest of his own good deeds, heaved up on the shore of lost illusions.

A bunch of crooks, all of them. His father, the Czech stutterer, rising up from within him. *Crooks.* But he said the word not in fury, just shaking his head at the wonder of it. His voice held in its calm the unshed tears of how things *are.* This recognition wasn't a moment for the puny theatrics of personality, taking a stand, preening his own better character, *getting out.*

From this I came to see obliquely that my dreams of escape were delusions too. True, New York was more exciting, more—well, *more.* And Paris was out there somewhere. But what, as a girl, I wanted from the Great World Out There was not happiness or beauty. I was looking for trouble. The *filth* my mother wished to skirt as we passed Birdie's Market. The world was *so sad, so sad*—I wanted to get where that misery-inducing action was. Not that I wanted to be unhappy, but I wanted proximity to danger, to significance, to something *happening.* I held to the deep Midwestern faith: that life is elsewhere. That's where I wanted to be—elsewhere.

St. Paul's surface was smooth and brittle. It cracked like black ice beneath us here in the land of lakes. Keep the friends of your youth. Stay with your family. *People like us don't divorce,* he said with resignation, astonishing me another time in the truth-mobile of the Buick after a particularly furious harangue from my mother that left him, as usual, more dismayed than angry.

Add nothing, go nowhere, keep the same job, the same once-sweet, now-bitter wife, keep the same faith. He even said, more than once, *Why go to Minneapolis?* Everything you sought—danger, beauty, trouble enough—will come of its own accord. It will be all the more harrowing for happening here in the transcendent Nowheresville where it is least expected. The middle, the safety zone where he and my mother thought they lived. Elsewhere, it turns out, is right here. It'll come and get you, you with your fist in your pocket.

Thus in all disappointments he turned back, bruised, to the radiant origins of his belief in people and the essential rightness of the world. Justice, writ in gilt on the Cathedral dome, held existence aloft. Maybe this belief, the refusal to rage or rail, is the spiral of wonder and wounds that accounts for the bravery of supposedly ordinary people in allegedly ordinary lives.

Him, for example. My mild father holding his baggie of meds, who will shamble into the clinic where he is admired for his smile, his uncomplaining graciousness. One of the living obits who, "after a long courageous battle"—*dot dot dot.*

This courage isn't new to him. Death and dying are just the current theater of this plot in which the ingenue (him this time—I'm the mordant observer now, an ingenue emerita) never turns to sardonic stone. He has been, all these years, a gentleman in training to those he served with roses and Christmas trees, Fraser fir garlands, spring gardens and summer window boxes, the fantasy decor of beautiful party rooms. He wouldn't think of complaining.

But as we drive to his doctor, in the mobile confessional, he's been caught harboring a dark and disloyal thought. *I thought I'd be, you know...on my own.*

Still, he's mystified about where she has gone. Where is she, the pretty girl with the high cheekbones who walked into a classroom at Mechanic Arts High School in 1934 and saw him surrounded by the fast set? Fastened on him. The girl with her shy smile and dazzled, short-sighted baby blues. The girl he allowed, in time, to adore him. Who, unbelievably, went on to become what she is now: *quite a handful.*

ON THIS DAY, the last of the doctor visits I'm able to dredge up from memory, I pull the Buick into the dark cave of the parking garage of Midway Medical. I steer my father along the carpeted hallway to Internal Medicine, get him seated, check him in, remember to get the parking ticket stamped, sit down and pick up a tattered copy of *Real Simple*. My father thumbs through *Field and Stream*. In half an hour, an hour, who knows—his name will be called and we'll jump, as if it were a surprise to be seeing the doctor, as if we'd only come here to page through old magazines. There is a sign on the front desk:

PLEASE INFORM US
IF YOU HAVE BEEN WAITING
MORE THAN 15 MINUTES.

But we never inform them. I get caught up in *Real Simple*. He snoozes. Time passes. We live in eternity.

I'm irked when I hear his name called. I was coasting along, deep in an article offering ingenious tips about cleaning-product storage I want to finish. But my father is already up, toddling uncertainly toward the nurse, galvanized as usual by social responsibility, radiating his gentle smile. *I'm just fine, and how are you?*

He teeters slightly on the scale. He's lost weight—again. A joke: the one good thing about this, don't have to worry about my weight. Grins. The nurse laughs—that's a good one. *Oh, Stan!* The way the Summit Avenue matrons used to cry in appreciation.

Then we're alone in the examining room, me wedged in the corner chair, him perched on the examining table. Neither of us has a magazine in here. We just sit. My father looks at his hands as if they might have information.

Do you have anything you want to ask the doctor? I say in my day-care-provider voice.

Nope.

What about the itching?

He shrugs.

A tap on the door and the doctor bustles in. *Ah, you're here again—good,* he says, seeing me in the corner.

He helps my father take his shirt off. The birdie rib cage is exposed, the frail withers of his back, the flaccid taffy of his upper arms. My strong father in this weakling's body. The doctor taps, listens, moves around the body, tapping and listening. Then his hand on a swollen ankle, looking at the second hand on the wall clock, counting.

Then it's time to hand over the baggie of meds. The doctor lines up the little plastic containers on the desk. Stares at them, frowns, checks them against what he has written on the chart. I wait for him to say, "I have some more tricks up my sleeve, Stan."

But he looks up—at me. And then turns to my father. "We can get you on hospice now, Stan," he says as if he's offering to upgrade him to business class.

My father has been looking down and he doesn't look up. Doesn't search for a face—the doctor's, mine—where he might cast his fear or disappointment. He keeps looking at his hands as if they were two little fellow faces he carries around for companionship.

"Hospice," he says, trying it out. Then, looking up, he turns to me and says firmly, "I'd rather buy a Buick."

We gather up his meds in the baggie. We drive straight from Midway Medical to the Walser dealership on University. He holds the big glossy Le Sabre brochure he picked up on an earlier visit.

He's not going to get silver-gray this time, he says. Try something different. *This one*, he says, pointing to the color sample. Why not go for the gold-dust?

Chapter 9

HE DIED THE LAST DAY of November, the week after Thanksgiving. The gold Buick was barely six months old. The dealership was decent (a Stan word) about taking it back.

Toward the end, the social worker from the clinic found a live-in hospice with a free bed in a western suburb. But Leo the Lion was barely out of the "care facility" herself after one of her episodes—was it a stroke or a seizure? A stray fact I've lost over time, swirling somewhere in the downward spiral of all their medical episodes.

It was impossible to think of ferrying her back and forth to the suburb where the hospice was located. Her inner clock was smashed and she would want to be there at all hours. Her querulous voice insisting just in order to insist, to impose authority, an evicted chatelaine claiming sovereignty over her lost estate. *There's a great deal to do on the Archive.*

I resisted taking him to a suburb whose name meant

nothing, one of the mushrooms that had emerged, as if overnight, like flimsy fairy rings around the city, places that used to be wetlands, good waterfowl habitat, mallards, teals, good for fishing sunnies. Eagan, Woodbury, Burnsville, wherever they were, exits off the swooping freeways he never got used to. *This used to be a nice town. Before they cut it up.*

It wasn't exactly that I wanted him to die at home. He didn't think of the condo as home anyway even though Napoleon and Benito had followed them there, looking like ousted strongmen from another regime in forced exile in the modern building. Besides, he'd come to the edge so many times in any number of hospital rooms, in ERs, once on a trip to Iowa, in a medical helicopter thwacking its way back to St. Paul from Des Moines. But I didn't want him to die on the edge of the urban nowhere, the anonymous sprawl, he who had lived in the middle of St. Paul all his life and had only strayed across the bridge the last year of his life, to the condo in an old bluff area called Lilydale, as if he'd chosen for his last residence a deeper floral precinct.

So I managed to keep him at home—not "home," but at the condo. Round-the-clock nursing aide, hospice nurse every day, people in and out. Mother holding his hand. Peter came too, in from the West Coast at the end, saying firmly, *It's okay, Dad, you can let go now.* And my alarm—Don't say *that!*

He was past words. But he'd never been a big talker. Let him just stay here. Stay. Don't say it's okay to let go. He might get better. People get better. Amazing turnarounds. You read about it. Look at Mother.

All right, don't look at Mother. The big watery blind eye, the flyaway hair, desire whittled down to cigs and Chardonnay, the beatific smile flickering on and off. But holding his hand, not letting go.

The absolute unreality of the situation. Grief not as sadness but as a form of disorientation.

We sat around eating popcorn, waiting. The nursing aide was a large doughy woman who radiated goodness and was paid minimum wage, no health insurance—*I couldn't afford somebody like me if it was my turn.* She loved popcorn, and suddenly it was all I wanted to eat. The white food of my furious skinny teenage years. She called him Stany and sang as she sponged him down, the water sluicing over his collapsed flanks. *Okay, Stany, we're going to turn you now, my boy. Patricia, you take that side. One, two, three, alley-oop!*

Then, a Monday morning a couple of weeks into this, and the hospice nurse suggested I should go to the drugstore to get something called a scopolamine patch to put behind his ear. It would make his breathing easier, she said.

My brother shrugged. *Sure, go get it if you want to,* he said.

Later he told me the patch made no difference to Dad. *They do it for the family, so you don't have to hear the wet breathing.*

Wet breathing?

The death rattle, he said.

A term I associated with the Irish, all the wakes we'd gone to, the cakey faces on satin, the replay of end-scenes—*It was peaceful.* Or sometimes, alarmingly, the opposite—*She didn't want to go. She fought. They had the priest, but she was fighting.*

But thinking it would ease his pain, pain he no longer had, it turned out, I tore out the door to get the patch. On the way back to the condo, just as I was on the bridge over the Mississippi, my cell phone rang. My brother: *Get back here fast.*

Not fast enough. As I opened the door, Peter said, he took his last breath. *You missed it. Sorry, you missed it.*

I walked into the little bare bedroom with the rented hospital bed, and mother turned, still holding his hand, her big bleary eyes behind her thick glasses searching for my face. *It was a privilege,* she said without drama, the voice of a seer.

I didn't understand if she meant that being with him at the end was a privilege, or if she was trying to say their whole life together, or simply he himself, had been the immense honor that gave her voice that regal authority.

For days I had been urgently murmuring *I love you, I love you* into his ear. A charm against *letting go.*

But she got it right. Sat and held his hand, no airy nothings, just that final benediction, a perfect elegy.

And Peter, who'd been all those years on the West Coast, who didn't have the gift of gab—he got it right too. Stood at the side of the bed and said with almost military formality, *Thanks, Dad. Thanks.*

The Commandment isn't to love them. It's to honor them. *Thanks, Dad, thanks.*

And then, Peter said, he just went.

Out the bedroom window you could see the confluence of the Mississippi and the Minnesota rivers, brown and blue. A chevron of Canada geese was headed south, honking, a basso note floating over the flyway. Two men sat in a boat directly below the window, faced away from each other, silent, their lines in the water, waiting for a nibble.

He was buried in weirdly warm weather. Minnesota, December third, and temps in the 60s, as if the growing season were extending its condolences. None of the flowers froze at the grave site. A sign, I said to Leo the Lion, using her language, pointing to the roses.

She shook her head impatiently. The little people were off duty. Signs were no comfort. What was I thinking of?

IN THE SPRING, I went to the Czech hall on West Seventh for a reception in honor of Vaclav Havel who was visiting a local college, giving a talk about building a civil society. The local Czech Sokol club managed to claim him for an hour to visit the old brick hall where my grandparents had courted, where Saturday nights they had danced and played cards. Their world was the nineteenth century, and they kept it going in that hall and in their lives past the middle of the twentieth.

And even beyond that, beyond them. The local Czech Americans showed up in force for the evening, some of them tricked out in bright nineteenth-century peasant gear, speaking a Czech so antique that linguists on Fulbright exchanges now come over from Prague and Olomouc to study it.

The building was next door to St. Stanislaus Church where I was baptized, not far from the greenhouse, just up from the brewery, along the route of Frankie's funeral procession where all the workers had lined up on West Seventh as the cortege passed on the way to St. Stan's.

The main part of the hall held an auditorium with a proscenium-arch stage. A theatrical backdrop, painted sometime in the 1920s, was unfurled on the stage: Prague and the Vltava in a foreshortened perspective, the Hradcany slightly a-kilter. The place was crammed—a children's dance group, an adult dance group, and the eager and curious just wanting a glimpse of the great man. The program included country dances and Czech folk songs. Havel, onetime hipster, looked on neutrally. He bowed gravely and smiled shyly when one of the peasant girls handed him a bouquet.

He was bundled off to his next event, but the party went on. People crowded toward the kitchen area for beer and coffee, sausages and kolaches. My grandparents' generation were long gone, my father's going. He and my mother hadn't come for dances. All this was the past and I thought how distant I was from it, in the end.

I was about to leave, but as I turned to the stairway, I heard my name called. A woman, advancing across the creaking wood-plank floor, held her arms wide open. She rushed toward me in her bright red and black embroidered costume, a figure I vaguely registered from a distant childscape. She wasn't a long-lost relative, not an old neighbor, but I recognized her in the way I seemed to recognize everybody in the room, not by name or face but as resistant nubbins of the worn immigrant fabric of this low-rent neighborhood by the brewery (now an ethanol plant) where I was born.

She swept toward me, weighty mascara and boldface brows writ with a firm hand above the snapping dark eyes. She had to be eighty at least, but her floss of blond hair was still in the game, the smocked blouse open to a wink of cleavage.

So, she wasn't from my life but from my father's, his generation. And thinking this—*his generation*—it came to me that he had once taken her to a dance. Once. He mentioned this whenever (rarely) we encountered her, the dance offered as a winner's trophy to my mother: once was enough with that one—his soft grin, her smoky *ha-ha!*

And hearing this, my brother and I would bask, without comprehending the vastness of our comfort, in the billowing luxury of this union we understood never would, never could be put asunder, the marriage of our high-school-sweetheart parents trailing clouds of fidelity. A lock. And we the treasure secure within its stronghold.

We were so secure, it was suffocating. I used to wish idly that they *would* divorce. Not because they fought. Because I was looking for an out. Divorce, the rhododendron ranch in Argentina, a walk-up in Greenwich Village, Paree where the

FTD orders went in the dead of the night. Anything, anything. Somewhere, anywhere.

The woman's name refused to surface, but she knew mine and sang it out, first in English and then, ratcheting up our ethnic intimacy, cooed my name in stagy Czech, *Vlasticko, Vlasticko!* Then she had me, the wattled hammocks of her upper arms fastening me for a fond moment, pinned against the coffee-and-cake table while the crowd surged around us.

She was saying, as she held me, how sorry she was to hear of my father's death. She was out of town at the time—a cruise. This improbable word here on West Seventh— cruise—hovered between us for a prideful instant. She would have come to the funeral except for the cruise. She mentions Frankie's funeral, which she *did* attend.

In St. Paul, this remark does not strike either of us as strange. Nor do I feel foolish thanking her for having come to my uncle's 1936 funeral, long before I was born and baptized at St. Stan's, same church he was buried from, next door to the Czech hall where we now stand in this timeless embrace.

This woman, onetime date of my father, belongs to all that, the St. Paul that erases the suburbs and the sprawl, the bully river town that was hypnotized by other people's wealth, their exhilarating rise (the Empire Builder!), and in yet deeper solidarity to hardship and the bracing memories of their own hardscrabble lives (*We put lard on our bread!*), as well as baffled wonder at the thought of how both the grandeur and misery had disappeared as if they had never been, lost now in the muddle of a middle-class pension that allows even this elderly child of West Seventh to go on a winter cruise in the Caribbean.

She had never moved away. "I'm always here," she said. It wasn't clear if she meant she was always at the Czech hall or that she had remained in the old neighborhood. Still here, still enduring the sting of peroxide for the greater civic good. Still a girl I cannot imagine my father...dating. Though even now, lost in space as she is, it's easy to see my mother lifting an unpainted eyebrow at this Old World goose girl: *What a getup, who does she think she's kidding?*

The whole neighborhood, she tells me, attended Frankie's funeral, the men with their hats off, lined up the length of West Seventh as the cortege left St. Stan's. Mr. Bremer, owner of the brewery, wept right there on the public street. "Your grandfather," she says, lowering her voice as if confiding an indecency, "kept asking *why* Frankie, why not *him*. He wanted to die." Another one wanting to die—Mother, the Czech grandfather, the Irish grandfather actually accomplishing the deed, turning to the wall.

She has released me, but keeps my hand captive in both of hers that flash with rings and bright polish. "He sobbed and sobbed at Kessler's," she says, naming the neighborhood funeral home. "He wanted to *die*."

She hands this over, a relic she's been keeping in the vault of memory like a faithful retainer who can now pass on the family silver to its rightful heir. I've heard this story all my life—from my grandmother, my aunts and older cousins, though my father never indulged in these recitations, these jags of sentiment about my uncle and my sobbing grandfather, the stuttering concertina player.

Out of some strange mixture of embarrassment and courtesy, I manage to look surprised for the benefit of this Czech Mae West. I pretend my grandfather's depth of grief is news to me. She pats my arm.

"And how is your mother doing?"

A canny look passes over the woman's bright face. *And how is your mother doing?* At first I think she knows—but how?—the litany of my mother's woes, the strokes and seizures, the frets and furies, the midnight prowlings in her bathrobe along the corridors of the condo building. The condo manager who says I must "do something" about her. "She frightens the others." Ah yes, *the others*, all the white heads in the decorous no-pets building who wonder which of them will be next, patrolling the insomniac halls, the coiled strands of their long careful lives suddenly unspooling madly. Like hers.

But this woman regarding me from under the sticky lattice of her lashes has no such clairvoyant bead on my mother in spite of her searching look. She's just asking how my mother is handling the death of my father only a few months ago. The death she missed because of her cruise to the islands.

I tell her it's hard (of course) but she's managing (of

course). This is the right answer, if not quite the true one, and she nods, the blond floss dipping in assent.

"Was he buried out of St. Stan's?" she asks.

Here I cannot please her. "St. Luke's," I say, naming the parish of the solidly middle class to which we had ascended, up the hill, away from the brewery and the greenhouse, a breach of loyalty to West Seventh (*I'm always here*). She nods, allows it. "You moved up the hill, didn't you?" she says as of a region beyond a mountain range of which she has heard rumor. "Your mother was from up there, wasn't she?"

My mother often elicited this slight annoyance—from my aunts, my cousins. My mother who, even now, would roll her china-blue eyes at the flossy peasant girl who holds my hand. Do they take her for a snob? For I sense in this disapproval a wounded response to a more resistant disapproval that my mother radiates, has always radiated, to the polka dancers, the wearers of flouncy dresses, the peroxiders and mascara-appliers of the world. She will stay home and reread the *Letters of Flannery O'Connor*, thank you very much.

"She was from the Cathedral," I say, using the old St. Paul geographical shorthand.

"Did he die at home?" she asks.

"Yes," I say, and hear the pride in my voice that I managed this. But I don't say that *home* was not the house of fifty years "up there," but a condo they moved to barely a year before across the river, not even in the city limits. I let her think he died "up there." I seem to be protecting her, as if this second remove away from West Seventh would be a greater betrayal. Of what?

But now she is saying my father was such a handsome man. I'm used to this. He had that allure for the women of his generation, even into old age. I grew up hearing my mother's girlfriends murmur admiration. "We all thought he was so handsome," she says again.

But she has glimpsed someone in the crowd and drops my hand, calling out, "Herm, Herm—over here!" And Herman Vacek, onetime city councilman from West Seventh during the sixties, bounds over (*What a gasbag*, Leo the Lion always said in her take-no-prisoners way whenever we ran into him). Still a man to work a room, he kisses Evelyn. "Ain't she something?" he asks no one in particular and Evelyn, on cue, tosses her blond head and laughs. A woman still glad of admiration, which I notice does make her appear younger.

I like her, I can't help it. I like the mascara and the dyed hair. She's having fun. Why not? Leo the Lion never dyed her hair, went gray, then yellowy white. *Who am I trying to kid?*

Then Herm Vacek is on to me, his eye uncertain at first, but then focused, slowing down to kindliness. "Stan's daughter?" he asks, and takes my hand as Evelyn did, in both of his, a gesture of condolence. "I was sorry to hear about your dad," he says. "What a gentleman."

My hand jerks away from the big gentle mitts, against my will. I'm startled at the dart of disdain I feel toward this man, this *gasbag* (stop it, Mother), standing here in arrogant good health, commenting on my father's character, his beer belly lolling over his belt buckle, an affront to trim, and finally frail, Stan. He's the one who should have heart problems. The refreshments area is filling up with people, and Herm doesn't seem to notice my rudeness. I've been unfair, and I feel ashamed. But no harm done, apparently. He's off to another group across the room, glad-handing as if he were still up for reelection.

But Evelyn noticed. She has drawn closer to me again, some urgency in her face. There are people crowding around us, toward the table with all the food. But even before she speaks, as if my mother's spooky Irish clairvoyance had invaded me, I sense an intensity, a wire binding us, separate from everything around us in the hall.

"I don't know," she says. And hesitates. But then goes on in a rush. "The last time I saw your father, it must have been five years ago. Mrs. Jindra's wake."

A name I remember, another speck of West Seventh dust, another of their generation.

"Your mother wasn't there. You mother, maybe she wasn't well. I don't know. Your mother wasn't always well. Your father was there. He came by himself. So handsome, as always. Always dressed so nice, wore a tie. So many don't wear a tie anymore."

I can tell she is looking for a way out, that she has launched herself into deep water and is grasping for a life ring.

She looks at me for an instant as if I might help her out of this. All of this is palpable, but the movie keeps rolling.

"We walked out of the funeral parlor together, your father and I," she says. "He said something and we were laughing. Jokey and friendly. I don't remember what it was about." She seems troubled about this lapse, as if it might explain something.

"And he was walking me to my car, we were walking and my car was ahead a couple of rows, and I asked him how your mother was," she says. "I was telling him about my husband's heart attack and that he was better. And then I asked about your mother. I always asked about your mother."

She stops dead. I bend my head nearer.

Why did I do that? I probably urged her over the edge.

"And your father said, he just said right there, he said, *You're the one I should have married.*"

She looked at me in horror, the yellow fleece of her hair an alarm around her face, eyebrows perched in dismay. Who knows how I looked to her. It felt as if our faces were almost touching.

"I just ran. I ran and ran as fast as I could to my car. I didn't turn around till I got to my car. I was just shaking."

At the far end of the table Herm Vacek was slapping the back of a man with a huge beer belly, as big as his own, two great Czech beer barrels by the table groaning with food.

Chapter 10

HE SHOULD NEVER have bought the business. I think we all knew that. Eventually even he admitted it ("I should have been ten years younger..."). But to pass up the chance of making it his own would have been like not marrying the girl of your youthful dreams even if she came to you too late, broken-down and haggard. Your girl's your girl. Another Scott Fitzgerald sentiment.

The company had been established in the robber-baron days of the late nineteenth century by two Swedish immigrants who had strayed from Minneapolis over to St. Paul. The second and third generations of these family owners were in charge of the business during my girlhood. This was a lengthy pedigree in the Midwest—a company with its centenary within sight.

This heritage meant that my father, as manager of both the greenhouse and the downtown store, was part of *history*, the third aspect of the Trinity I held sacred—beauty, the idea of elsewhere, and the holy ghost of history. Even my mother, house historian who held no brief for the flower trade, grudgingly allowed that the firm was indeed "historical." It had always been *the* florist to the carriage trade, she said. We used that term—carriage trade—as if it still meant something. In old St. Paul it did. Not until the freeways cut their gashes across St. Paul and Minneapolis in the late sixties was the stiff back of the little provincial city broken. And maybe not even then. Maybe not now.

The greenhouse strayed over a city block in the Czech neighborhood where I was born and where some of the growers lived. The small houses of the neighborhood were etched at the narrow sides and cubed backyards with fastidious gardens. All summer long there was much pickling and "putting up" of vegetables and fruits. In the fall, when it was time to change from screens to storm windows, people laid a screen or two on bricks on the back porch to dry the mushrooms they had gathered in the woods by the river. These were people who really would have felt better if they could keep their own chickens.

The greenhouse was cut up into dozens of linked houses. There was, as well, a separate barn where Christmas trees were stacked, and during the unfortunate fifties and sixties, were flocked pink or blue. A bulb cellar was cut into the earth below the cement walkway connecting the houses. A dim lightbulb on a string at the top of narrow stairs led the way

down, down to this netherworld. When I read of the cata-
combs in school, the bulb cellar sprang so powerfully to mind
that I felt an eerie shiver of time travel. I had experienced the
licking fires of hell at the open door of the boiler room, and
my nostrils quivered with the dank molder of martyrs amid
the buried tulips.

Each house was dedicated for parts of the year to a different range of plants, a broad array of indoor and outdoor vari-
eties. The geranium house in spring became, by December,
the first poinsettia house. The poinsettias were secretly growing much of the summer, unnoticed and unwanted, in a back
house, the same house that took in the geranium cuttings in
their off-season.

There was even a house for special customers to leave
their plants to "winter over" while they themselves were win-
tering over in Florida or Arizona. Shaggy aspidistras and leggy
geraniums, woody tree roses with name tags—Mrs. Ordway,
Mrs. Schultz—were lined up like elderly boarders in the first
greenhouse, near the design tables where cut-flower arrangements and corsages were made up.

The palm house, with an especially high glass roof, had big
dusty palms that lived for decades like old circus elephants,
rented out for weddings and charity balls and the theater and
opera productions that came through town from New York
and Chicago. The orchids were kept in harem seclusion behind a trellis with passion vines trained up one side in little-
visited house 11, up the steep hillside.

Charity balls, weddings, debutante parties, the private conservatories that became a sudden fashion in the seventies—there was much of set design to the business. One Easter Saturday my father worked through the night, jamming cut lilies into chicken wire formed in the shape of a massive cross fastened to the soaring wall of Gloria Dei Lutheran Church. On Easter morning the astonished Lutherans were greeted by this unearthly *oeuvre*, the gigantic risen cross of blossoms floating before them, bearing the overpowering scent of ripe lilies. The *Pioneer Press* put it on the front page.

The greenhouse itself may have encouraged my father's Cecil B. DeMille tendencies. It was the kind of glass greenhouse rarely found anymore, not stocked with a single crop like the massive cost-efficient warehouses now in favor but spilling over in many glass rooms with a little of this, a little of that, a single row of pineapple geraniums, a flat of mixed freesias, a low trailing bundle of damp mosses and maidenhair fern for shade gardens, a sudden riot of rock garden moss roses.

During "spring rush," when everyone was garden-crazed, this house was crowded with celery-and-white and port-streaked caladium, expensive annuals favored for shade gardens of Crocus Hill. For several years, a canny robin made its nest in the house just off the design room. The growers moved around gingerly in this area. They finally transferred all the plants to another house, so the mother wouldn't be nervous. During this period the greenhouse cats were sequestered in the lunchroom, howling at the injustice. But the growers kept the door firmly shut. Even in paradise the peaceable kingdom needed policing.

IN THE END—or too near the end—he bought the company. It was not what is called a wise business decision. The company had been skidding along on its antique carriage-trade reputation for decades, and for a long time hadn't been a healthy venture. Before the first generation had passed, feuding had become a company tradition. Complicated buyouts of distant family members weighted the annual balance sheets, and there was much bad blood.

The best years for the business, my father said, had been the war years, before my time. All the GIs sending flowers to their girls—their girls and their mothers. Nothing else to spend money on.

The first owners, known by their initials—A.B. and O.L.— had adjoining desks in the greenhouse office, and managed for something over thirty years never to speak to each other. They wrote notes or used their sons or employees for communication purposes. *This is to note that half a gross of roses from Florida . . . I hope someone will convey to O.L. the information that the Holland tulip market . . .*

Their picture was on the wall of the greenhouse showroom, two portly men dressed in pre–Great War fussbudget attire, uncannily alike, a Tweedledee and Tweedledum of floristry, one on either side of a horse that was tethered to a boxy wagon with the company logo scrolled across it, big wicker baskets of flowers wedged between great cubes of ice flecked with sawdust. The two men stared ahead. The horse too stared ahead, a diplomatic beast keeping the peace. During the Depression, after my father came to work in the greenhouse just out of high school, A.B. began "doctoring." He even went to the Mayo Clinic in Rochester. He came back from Mayo, briefly, and went through the greenhouse, shaking hands with every grower and worker, including my father who was then low in the pecking order, mixing manure into soil in the back garage area.

A.B. was going back to Mayo, he said, for an operation, something called a lobotomy. He'd come to say good-bye. "When it's over, I won't be myself anymore," he said.

When he came back from the operation, he wandered through the greenhouse, my father said, and it was true he wasn't himself. He wasn't anybody at all.

The middle generation, ten or fifteen years older than my father, carried on the chilly partnership during my girlhood. These were the owners I knew, the one I saw as a playboy, the other a cold fish, both of them having the wary looks of Mafia dons who watch their backs.

With his unerring weakness for a gallant Fitzgerald hero, my father sided with the playboy with the heart of gold who came from the weaker side of the partnership. I would have picked him too. Rolf wasn't blond—he was golden. He gleamed with good spirit.

Unlike my father, Rolf's association with the Summit Avenue world was not wholly one of service: he belonged to the same clubs, was seen at the same restaurants, owned a cabin on the right lake, lived in a big house a block off Summit.

His blue eyes widened with gladness to see you. He would say, "Ice cream?" as a greeting, and rush to the freezer where he kept his stash. He shared my father's joie de vivre, except for him it was a birthright, easy and natural, not the responsibility of a faithful servant assigned to be master of revels.

He treated my father well. He was the first person, my father said, to treat him "like a gentleman." Whatever that meant. But it did mean something to him; it was the gold standard of his measure of a man. Rolf was his beau ideal. He would do anything for Rolf.

Leo the Lion shook her head: *a drinker* was her verdict, speaking from her Irish authority, though Rolf could charm her too, given a chance—*Mary, darlin', aren't you something tonight!*

My father covered up any number of Rolf's high jinks and troubles, his late appearances, his complete absence. He even tried to take over his bookwork, going back to the greenhouse late at night to see if he could get things on track. "What does Rolf *do* down there, anyway?" my mother asked. She claimed he was walking around with gin in his coffee mug at ten in the morning.

I never told them what Rolf's daughter said. Celeste, a string bean with a fall of golden hair that looked like a stream of honey from a jar. We were together at their lake place, the two of us contentedly pouring salt from a Morton's box over leeches we'd caught and laid on the dock, one of those contemplative cruelties of childhood, the inky bloodsuckers writhing without a sound. "My father owns your car," she said out of nowhere. "And your house. My father owns everything you have."

This was not the remark of a gentleman. I knew that. I kept pouring salt, the shiny black creatures curling and withering under the blizzard I hurled from on high. *What are you doing?* my father said, frowning, reaching to take the Morton's box.

Nothing, Rolf's daughter said sulkily, and grabbed the salt away before he could take it. She went on pouring.

Eventually it was impossible to protect Rolf. He cried when he called my father into his knotty-pine office off the main showroom. He had to sell his share of the business to "the other side," he said. The big house a block off Summit— gone. He was moving to Florida where he was getting a job with a big rose-growing outfit. "These wholesale places are the future, Stan."

Rolf with a *job*? Rolf wasn't an ordinary person who got a job—he had a *place*. And of course there was the matter of Florida—Florida was Siberia with high temps, Mars, another universe. Even for me, always sniffing for the escape hatch, it sounded grim. Wholesale was dark, forbidding, all business. We were in retail where the people were, the sparkling spenders.

Rolf was gone forever.

A lot of the fun went out of the greenhouse when Rolf left, taking his glamour, blue eyes, and his afternoon ice cream to the Gulf Coast where he did not prosper. My father continued to worry about him, and years later he covertly sent him a check now and again "just to tide him over."

Leo the Lion shrugged.

My father was left in the employ of Harold, son of the other founding family, who seemed a soul-soured bottom-liner with no apparent love of flowers. This troubled my father, but Harold let him run the greenhouse and the shop. Let him. That was how we saw it—my father was allowed to run the show, keep things going in the downtown show-room and the Banfil Street greenhouse, maintaining the ever changing storefront window displays, keeping the customers charmed and cosseted.

We didn't think of this arrangement, where Harold didn't "interfere" and where my father did all the real work, as a matter of exploitation, so persuaded were we by his own love affair with the greenhouse. Harold rolled in at eleven, in time for lunch downtown at the Athletic Club, then turned up again around three to check the day's receipts, and then it was out for drinks at the Lowry before five. He had a desk some-where, and sometimes sat at it, calling his broker, speaking low into the receiver. He always seemed distracted. You got the feeling he was a little startled to see all these flowers around, as if he leapt over the irritating intermediate steps of the business to the essential point of it all: the money.

Also a drinker, according to my mother. He seemed narrow, without curiosity, and you didn't really know if he was pickled much of the time. He started talking about moving to California. The business was changing—grocery stores were selling bunches of flowers in plastic pails for a couple of bucks! And people were buying them!

He wanted out. The company was bleeding. They offered it to my father, the aged and broken beauty he had loved all his life.

He didn't hesitate. They left to him, along with the old greenhouse and the shop downtown, various ancient encumbrances, and rumors of financial irregularities.

Then, finally in possession of his beloved, my father turned the other cheek, and several years later was embroiled all over again in problems with his new business partner. The taxman came to the door, that boogeyman of imperiled small businesses. The heart attacks started.

When it became patently evident that his younger partner preferred investing in more profitable land outside of town rather than tending the greenhouse and store as my father thought he should, and my father lay in United Hospital, wheezing while the cardiologist managed, once again and for a while longer, to drain fluid from his congested heart, his only fury—a brief but bitter rage—was at my brother and me when he discovered we had hired a lawyer to pursue his rights. *A guy has to do the right thing, no matter what the other guy is doing . . .*

It turned out we weren't living in a Fitzgerald novel after all. This was Dickens, complete with threatening letters on legal letterhead, the gallant dying hero betrayed by advantage-taking villains, generations of cynical venality twisting the plot, and even our very own Uriah Heap who, after all, was a good guy. Nice smile, same Catholic schools, up the hard way. This was the sort of reasoning our father had given us as business acumen.

The heart attacks made retirement necessary not long after, and at first it seemed everything was going to be all right. No more second mortgages on the house to cover the winter heating bill at the greenhouse, no more tax inspectors coming to the house, and a regular check from Uriah Heap every month plus Social Security. Not bad. For a while.

Then we learned (from Leo the Lion) that our father, supposedly retired and out of the company, was taking out a second mortgage on their house and loaning the money to tide the business over, explaining that this made sense, that his partner needed a little boost. This seemed to work for a while, every winter a loan, and then as the spring planting season kicked in, he was repaid. But then, one winter, my father's voice on the telephone, low and embarrassed—their checking account was down to eleven dollars.

His partner wasn't able to keep up. He meant no harm—his point, the point my father urged on me too. The partner felt it needed to be explained to me. *Patricia, if you only knew what the flower business is like now. It's not like it used to be....* I stood in the greenhouse and stared at him with the dead eyes of Leo the Lion.

There were ingrates and phonies, wrongs to be righted, money owed that should be decently paid, and so forth. My brother and I—naturally—were on the side of the good, the true, the beautiful. Our father.

Who wanted no part of our crusade. "You don't *do* this," he wheezed from his hospital bed, trailing his oxygen, horrified that his partner had received a letter from a lawyer, thanks to us. He acted as if we were endangering peace on earth. I suppose we were.

His allegiance was not to the truth, not even to fair play, not even to Justice when it came to his own just claims. His loyalty went to the invisible silken net of human relations webbed with let-it-go shrugs that, every day, keeps the universe from clawing itself to death.

You behave a certain way, no matter what the other guy does, as all his life he mildly called those who did not abide by his form of rectitude. From his lard-eating, we-had-nothing boyhood on the wrong side of the tracks, from his half century of winters stoking the eternal springtime of the greenhouse, he had somehow fashioned an ethic befitting the Dalai Lama. No blame, no blame.

But you're being cheated, my all-business oral-surgeon brother said, to which I, bully with poetic righteousness, chimed along. My mother, her Irish heart always glad of a fight, encouraged us to pursue our *Bleak House* plots.

But in the end, I suppose it is accurate to say our father got his way: the lawyers said that there wasn't enough money to pursue the matter. He died with the balance of the money owed him never paid back, the ingrates and phonies gone their merry or regretful ways, thinking Stan was a good man with a vicious wife and unkind children. Poor Stan, they could say.

And poor us—they could say that, too. Here was a decent working man, trying to meet a payroll, misunderstood by his greedy, overeducated kids. They didn't understand anything. Just goes to show you.

AUNT LILLIAN WAS DEAD, and her protective husband, Bill, was gone, too. My favorite aunt. She once said with unembarrassed simplicity—I hadn't asked, she just came out with it—*Bill and I tried sex a couple times, but we decided we didn't like it. We just hug.*

Their careful lives were dismantled by the older nieces, the duplex on Jefferson sold. Lillian, fearful and watchful, who had so narrowly been saved from disaster, was gone, a lifetime after her twin, the magical Frankie, had been lost to her.

Something always uncertain in her eyes, a faint alarm or watchfulness in the tidiness of her overorganized closets, the massive use of Saran Wrap. A lot of loss in that life, I decided, or a lot of absence—no children, no sex, no diamond ring as a souvenir of her other half. But at the center of her life was that saving grace: how she had been plucked from disaster by her peasant mother, who ran out of the house in the nick of time, grabbed the chloroform rag from her face, and chased the rapist away before *the worst* could happen.

Wasn't it amazing, I remarked to my brother, how lucky that was—Nana saving Aunt Lillian from the rapist. Of course being *almost* raped had to be scary too.

"What are you talking about?" he said.

"How Aunt Lill was almost raped. Didn't you know?"

"Who told you that? She wasn't *almost raped*. She *was* raped. Some guy in the neighborhood."

The fantasias of the kitchen table, rococo descriptions festooning a life. The duplicitous double accounting, keeping two books—one story for the boy (he can take the truth), one for the girl (she must be protected).

The tumbler jigged in the lock, the heavy safe clicked open, my brother's truthful blue eyes that don't lie looking at me.

Our fearful aunt, checking the gas stove, her manicured finger touching each of the knobs to be sure the fire was off, off, off, counting her shoe boxes. *We decided we didn't like it. We just hug.*

I asked my brother who it was. The rapist.

Some guy in the neighborhood. They knew him, knew his family. That's why they didn't do anything about it. They were funny that way—they were all in it together. Peter shook his head. He's a forensic dentist, identifies the bad guys who do terrible things, the ones who leave bite marks. Another Justice man. *They covered it up. They were all together down there.*

But wasn't that when everything was right, when everybody was together? *Nobody had anything.* That meant everyone was equal, everyone was happy. The Supreme Court Justice came home from Washington and wanted what we had. Our Nothing Soup.

Another fiction unspooling at the kitchen table from the tight coil of the well-told tale.

THE GREENHOUSE CAME shattering down, and the land was sold to the city. Eminent domain. A freeway and "affordable housing" were built under the Summit Avenue bluffs where, for more than a century, the glass houses had run up the side of a hill to catch the slant of northern sun to best advantage.

It could even be said that my mother got a bit of what she treasured most—an abiding grudge against the villains and cheats of the world. And evidence that, in the end, her two children, the stolid boy and the headstrong girl, were united in the Irish grudge culture. She fondled this knowledge like a jewel in a velvet box while my father lived and even after he died, until her mind was taken from her.

Then she entered her final phase, the beatific dementia. All was forgiven in the obscuring fog of what was once her mind. The sharp corners of her grudges smoothed, softened. They disappeared like melted ice in springtime.

Before that, when we went to Ireland together, in Kilkenny, her ancestral town, I'd asked her what, as a girl, she'd wanted to be when she grew up. It was assumed that neither she nor my father had been allowed to choose their fate, their future. A sense of renunciation abraded their lives, the lives of their family and even most of their friends—cheerful renunciation. The Depression had decided everything.

Yet their deep absorption in their work, their gratitude for decent jobs, the palpable satisfaction, made it hard to remember that they had had dreams of something other. For him— the doctor, the architect. For her—a librarian, I assumed, a real one, not a file clerk at a library.

I carried the stiff inner pride of being the family rebel all my adult life. I'd gone against her, chosen my own way, sat in the street against the war, lived with the scruffy draft-resister boyfriend, got myself the arty life. Maybe I didn't get out of St. Paul, but I'd followed my dream, become a writer, the very thing I knew she thought would spell doom. *Wouldn't you rather be a librarian?*

But in the little room in the Kilkenny B and B, when I asked her what she'd wanted to be as a girl, she looked at me from her twin bed, tucked up in her cotton jammies, and said in disbelief, "You don't know?"

"No, what did you want to do?"

"Be a writer, of course. I always wanted to be a writer."

So there is no escape. Choice is an illusion, rebellion is a mad dash on a long leash. She smiled at me, a funny, wry smile. Showed her hand at last.

And I'd thought I was his girl.

You can't tell, sometimes for years and years, the English majors in Vincent Hall were told, who the great artists are. You think it's a celebrated someone, and then years later it turns out to be a writer who never even published—think of Emily Dickinson. You just never know who the true artist is in your own time, they told us. History decides.

The vast skeins of description she used to roll into a ball at the kitchen table unraveled eventually, returned to wooly fluff, to nothing at all. She became mine to take care of, she who masqueraded as the archivist, who turned out to be the writer. And like the real artists that History chooses, after her strokes and seizures and after Stan was gone, she entered at last the world that had been his, the supreme fiction where Justice and Mercy kiss, where the lion lies down with the lamb.

Chapter 11

LIKE EVERYONE, I became a busy person, especially after my father died and my mother's care fell to me. I frequently told people how busy I was, I e-mailed to several continents on the subject: I'm swamped, stressed, I'm at wits' end. It was my main message. But then it seemed to be everyone else's message too.

I toiled under the weight of tottering piles of paper, burdened by the unanswered correspondence of dusty decades, crushed by dumb domestic details, waking panicked in the unforgiving night, the dread of my sins of omission (mainly— I didn't have *time* for sins of commission) stabbing at my heart. Above all, I was laid low the past five years—make that closer to ten—by the nineteenth-century duties of middle-aged postmodern daughterhood invoked these days by the oily social-work term *primary caregiver.*

My typical salutation became the apology—I'm late, I'm

behind. Sorry, sorry, sorry. Much hand-wringing. There was grandiosity to it, as if everyone were waiting for me. Yet I couldn't stop the racing pulse, the clutch of the heart.

How did this happen to me, a person who never took an Incomplete in college, who was never late for the orthodontist in high school? I throw myself on the mercy of six or seven people daily. I am just terribly, terribly sorry much of the time.

On my birthday the first year after my father's death, I received as a gift a cookbook called *The Cake Bible.* I didn't waste a minute with it. Who has time to bake a cake? I put it on a shelf in the kitchen beside my other cookbooks with the intention that someday I would bake a cake, a truly beautiful cake.

This, in fact, was the purpose of *The Cake Bible* in my life as it has been the core use of all the cookbooks I have collected over the years. They are the Edenic beacons of the Someday of perfection and possibility. Their recipes are the scripture of a faith uniting Platonic form and chaotic human appetite in a transcendent communion I believe in passionately though there is no proof of its existence. These texts, fat and reassuring, roll with the authoritative impersonality of reference books.

Someday. All this will happen someday, when the deadlines have been met, the to-do lists checked off, when the piles of correspondence have been answered, when—this especially—my tiny, almost-blind mother, who has drifted these five years after my father's death in the ether of a (more or less) benign dementia, when all this has passed and little Mary is released to the heaven to which she claims to aspire.

Then, let there be cake.

She lived for almost a year at the condo after he died. Then to an "assisted living" building where I tried to sustain her "independence," but simply bought her deeper isolation in the faux "apartment" where the stove was never used, the second bedroom was a pretend office for the computer she had been so proud to command. The You've Got Mail ding still delivered ten or twelve Viagra ads a day. She thrilled to the sound of the bell, thinking people were writing her letters. "What's all this about a penis?" she said, baffled. "Is this smut?" Smut, filth, how did it manage to invade her world? She stopped going into that room.

Then came the day the manager of the condo said I had to "do something" about my mother who was swanning around the hallways in her nightie at two AM announcing to anyone who intercepted her that she was fine, thank you, just waiting for her daughter to pick her up for Mass at St. Peter's. Finally, another couple of falls and a broken hip later, the stage set of the assisted-living apartment was struck, and she was off to the Marian Center, a frank nursing home where, afternoons, I wheeled her outside for a cigarette.

But on a glorious day in May her last full year, I stopped between coffee and work, and picked *The Cake Bible* off the kitchen bookshelf. Maybe the attractive blasphemy of the title lured me or maybe it was the author's introduction, a severe science-y lecture on the chemistry of emulsion. But in truth, I think it was the pictures, an album of formal studio portraits of *perfect cakes*, each more impressive than the last. There, modest and without architectural ambition, claiming only half a page but all the more alluring for its apparent modesty, was a cake frosted the color of antique wedding satin. The butter cream was laid on like fresh stucco to a restored Hapsburg villa in old Austro-Hungary. The cake was named Lilac Nostalgia.

And here it was—lilac time. And lilacs my favorite of all flowers. Actually, a florist father would seem to work against a passion for lilacs. For lilacs, being practically wild, abundant, and free, are dismal failures as a retail commodity. But at this time of year, St. Paul, finally unfrozen, is always lilac-town. The lilac is our consolation prize, a post-winter badge of honor. The scent lies heavy in the mid-May air, it follows you home, it overcomes, for a scant week, the incense of ages in the musty Cathedral down the block where, a lifetime ago, Mary walked with her little white book down the aisle toward Stan who had decorated it with stephanotis. In mid-May lilac even overpowers the rank garbage cans along the narrow alleys of the Crocus Hill neighborhood where, it seems, the oldest, most profuse lilac canes flourish.

In *The Cake Bible* dozens of individual lilac blossoms had been painstakingly separated into distinct flowerets, and frozen in sparkling sugar, as if in deathless frost, each one affixed to the old-yellow walls of the Lilac Nostalgia cake like lavender stars caught up in the creamiest swath of the Milky Way.

The cake bore the straight-sided martial bearing that a slouching civilian cake of the sort I have always produced (slope-shouldered, its thin icing puddling on the cake plate) could never hope to achieve. The Lilac Nostalgia stood at attention, its lavender medallions fastened like so many medals for valor on its soldier chest. A cake in dress uniform, in service to a sweetness worth fighting for.

I COULDN'T GET IT out of my head—the antique yellow of the cake, the pale pink raspberry mousseline lying against the layered bosom of the cake like a silk chemise, creating, as the recipe put it, "a harmony of color and flavor." I kept thinking of the perfection of it all. Of the glistering lilacs. Of the words "lilac" and "nostalgia" together. I took to heart the advice of *The Cake Bible*'s author who said that while keeping commercial crystallized lilacs on hand was "nice" (the arch offhandedness of her damning), they could not hope to compare with the admittedly time-consuming but "dazzling" results of the hand-crystallized lilac.

And so I found myself at a strip mall of a distant northern suburb, in a cake-decorating store, buying a box of superfine sugar, a minute paintbrush, and a box of parchment paper, along with a big jar of powdered egg whites. Rose Levy Beranbaum, the author of *The Cake Bible* had said nothing of powdered egg whites. "This will last you," the clerk, a woman weighing something like 250 pounds, told me, holding out the jar. In the well-stocked aisles of the strangely medicinal-looking cake store, I listened raptly as she told me how to mix up the powdered egg whites with water. "You don't want real egg whites," she said, taking me firmly in hand, "you want to avoid any threat of salmonella."

"Baking," she said, "can be dangerous...It's all chemistry."

"Like love," I said, idiotically.

She was having none of this soft-mindedness. "There are some here who don't think much of *The Cake Bible*," she said darkly.

Back home, I set up my chem experiment in the kitchen. Past noon already, and the lovely spring weather had turned. It was no longer a cake-baking day. Barometric pressure way down to pancake-flattening numbers. Thunder cracked perilously near, comic-book lightning stabbed the sky. The big splashes of rain that precede a real soaker came down in languid strokes, marking the sidewalk in dark dashes.

I ran outside with my father's old florist knife with his name—STAN—etched in his own hand on the bone handle. I flicked it open like a switchblade, and made for the alley where lilacs lolled over a brick wall in heavy grapelike clusters. I hacked down armloads, and still the bushes looked untouched, so full of flowers were they, attesting to the bountiful nature of the lilac. The storm blew in as I worked. By the time I got inside again, the giant bouquet was drenched, the

lilacs were intensely fragrant, and the leaves which, as Whit-
man noted, are heart-shaped, were shining as if they had
been washed with egg white and only awaited a rain of sugar
to memorialize them fully.

I put the lilacs in vases, first clubbing the bottom of the
branches with a hammer as my father taught me so the water
could be drawn up the opened capillaries of the woody canes.
Then I settled into the kitchen in the strange early-afternoon
dark, deeply content, first pulling the lavender flowerets apart,
then painting dry egg white (though now wet—you add water
and whisk, and the powder does froth, just as the no-nonsense
woman in the cake store said it would) onto the little star blossoms, one by one, as the storm pounded down outside.

Time, somewhere between the blossom separating and
the egg-white painting, ceased to exist. The mind went empty
too, absent of urge or impediment, just dip, stroke, sugar, dip,
stroke, sugar, the blessedly brainless cycle of coating the flowers with the tiny brush, petal by eternal petal. The rain rained
down outside, the superfine sugar cascaded on the dampened
blossoms, the hours guttered away. I had no responsibilities,
no ambition. I wasn't a writer, not even a poet, and nobody's
daughter. I was alone with the lilacs, gilding them with glistening sugar in the drafty scriptorium of my kitchen.

I had all the time in the world.

BUT TIME, big mosquito with its sharp needle, comes zoning
in again for blood. Back to the real world of the late-afternoon

visit to the Marian Center, back to the life of contrition, the life of badly or barely honored love or duty—whatever this is that requires me to be there, be there.

I have my routine: grab the wineglass, the bottle of Chardonnay, check to be sure the Merit 100s and the Bic lighter are stowed in my purse. On the way over, I stop at the Greek restaurant where I have ordered a salmon Nicoise salad. Her favorite. I sometimes bring her this meal (or a BLT on toast—her other choice) instead of sitting with her in the dining room where the old women stare and clutch their baby dolls, amid the moaners and droolers of the third-floor Alzheimer's/dementia unit. Though, truth be told, I no longer feel alien in the dining room. Still, I am grateful that she is not a drooler, not a moaner. She's a floater, a vivacious chatterer. Good company, a favorite of the nurses and health aides. Of this, grasping at straws, I am proud.

It would not be quite accurate to say I like the place. But I feel at home there. I cannot explain this. I fought her move from the merely addled on the second floor to the in-orbit third floor. Before that, I fought the move from her assisted-living apartment to the nursing home. And before that from the condo to assisted living. And before that—well, there have been many stops on the downward spiral. *Treat her like a six-teen-year-old who's just crashed on her boyfriend's motorcycle.*

I squirmed and I quivered her first few days on third floor. I wept. Stan would have hated this, he wouldn't have let it happen.

It occurred to me he *should* have let it happen. It occurred to me that caring for her had done him in. *I thought I'd be, you know...on my own.* For a couple of last, sweet years, oil painting, violin playing.

But now, my kit of treats in my straw bag, I swing through the lobby, past the aviary with its bright songbirds, and up to third floor where not only my mother but, I sense, *her people* are to be found. I have with me, besides the wine, the salmon salad and the cigs, the requisite Chocolate Decadence brownie that I myself am unable to eat. It makes my eyes ache, but my mother crams them down every time with a delight so thorough I have to wipe off her messy little paws with a wet napkin afterward.

Today, as every day, she is astonished to see me. Where have I *been*? She, it proves, has been to Chicago where she was under arrest, though for nothing serious: I needn't worry. My father, dead these five final years of my daughterhood, has been difficult, she confides. She hopes I will go to him: he will listen to me, she says, magnanimously acquiescing to my greater powers.

Besides, there are other problems she must attend to. Her own mother, dead more than fifty years, simply will *not* speak to her. "Mother is very bad," she says with sorrow. This happens to old people, she reminds me. She shrugs. "There are a lot of people here who are not right," she says, lowering her voice out of courtesy, touching lightly the side of her head.

The way she touched it when I asked her if there was any

advance warning of her seizures. *There's a ticking.* "It's sad," she says now of the people who are not right. Her age-old message: *life is so sad, so sad.* Again the philosophical shrug. And then she beams me her beatific, free-as-a-bird smile.

This is a new smile, not the smile of her previous self, not a merely happy smile. It is a cosmic smile of vast dimension and knowing, and I'm beginning to think it may be the reason I cannot stay away.

People tell me I must get over my Catholic guilt—this is why I'm so determined to come here regularly, they say, though her own clock and calendar have been blown to smithereens and she doesn't track the regularity of my visits. *You don't need to go every day, she doesn't remember if you're there or not,* they tell me. Letting me off the hook.

She's glad of the picnic dinner. My original plan was to wheel her over in her chair to the park across the street, Indian Mounds Park overlooking the Mississippi, sacred ground. Some of the mounds have been fenced off in recent years, acknowledged at last for what they are: a cemetery.

But the rain ended that plan. I tell her we'll go to the coffee shop downstairs for dinner. There is no coffee shop, but I've fallen into the same fictional habits she has now: the lobby with a couple of small tables is "the coffee shop," the sidewalk entryway is "the terrace." I'm not aware of these fictions between us until I hear myself say them in front of one of the nurses who looks at me strangely.

I feed her like a bird so she doesn't have to hunt blindly

around her plate for the morsels of salmon. She doesn't need to be fed, but she smiles. "I like to be spoiled," she says. She opens her beak wide, helpfully. "It's good," she says of the poached salmon, "it's *wet*." She can reach for her wineglass herself, and she drains it with real thirst, like water.

"I love wine," she tells me, "but you don't need to worry, I won't get into drinking trouble." She who was in just that trouble for twenty years and beyond. The slurred evenings of bourbon and later "just a glass of white wine for me," laced with the phenobarb and Dilantin, the round-the-clock cocktail of all those years. My father saying, "We don't have to drink, Mary. Let's not drink. I don't care."

Good luck on that one, Dad. The beady eye glaring, the half gallon of Gallo in the fridge where the milk used to be.

Finally, my brother went behind her back (her bitter phrase) and got her doctor to reorder her meds. The doctor had been prescribing enough phenobarb and Dilantin for a Vikings linebacker, Peter said. He got no points for saving her life. I was a Goody Two-shoes, he was a meddler.

And yet, also: *I'm proud of you. Neither one of you ever gave us a minute's trouble.*

Not something I was able to take pride in.

Then, after the wine, the brownie, a two-handed operation. She wants to take it herself. She eats it all in a trice, licks her fingers. Then the cleanup, holding her small hands out for the wet towel I get from the bathroom, her wedding rings swiveling on her bony fingers.

Then outside, "on the terrace," because smoking is forbidden indoors. The rain has stopped and the air is buoyant, rinsed of the dark heaviness of the afternoon. Cake-baking weather again. "How about a smoke?" she says. I guide the Merit 100 into her blind hand that claws the distance between us for it. She puts it to her mouth and I snap the Bic lighter. She's good at this, a lifetime performing this gesture: pulling the drag deep into her soul, holding the sweetness there, and then, just when it seems it must have made its way past the curve of her bent spine and that even her toes are inhaling, she releases the sigh of smoke, almost mewing with relish.

"Are you tired?" I ask.

She is, she says. "I lead an exciting life," she says, "but all this traveling is tiring."

Then she beckons with a crooked finger. She has a secret. She needs to tell me something. "Sometimes the children don't approve," she says. She's been waiting all day on pins and needles to see what I'll say. Am I ready for a big surprise?

"Shoot," I say.

"I married Don today," she says. Naughty girl—waiting for the Goody Two-shoes daughter to be scandalized.

"Who's Don?" I ask.

She regards me with pity. "He's the owner of this *ship*," she says, once again astonished by this thick daughter. Then fretful, worried. "Do you mind? The children are often upset."

"No, it's okay," I say.

Then one of the little people inhabits me and I hear my-self saying, "Is he rich—Don?"

She looks at me with disdain. *"No! Not rich!"* she cries in revulsion. We're in the middle, don't I understand that? Not rich, not poor, just right. Whatever you do, never worry about money. Don't pay attention to it.

"Well, is he nice?"

"Oh, very nice," she says, purring at the comforting thought of her new husband.

But the little people can't resist. "As nice as Dad?" I ask.

She looks at me with her withering eyes, the big blank blind one and the wavering half-seeing one. She fastens me with a dart of outrage. "We don't compare anyone to Stan," she says.

I wanted her to say that.

I wheel her back to the elevator, up to third. Then I re-member the lilacs in the tinfoil package I've brought. They're good, according to *The Cake Bible*, "almost indefinitely." So I don't wheel her back to her room where Marie, her room-mate, always cries out to me, "Sister, Sister, what do I owe?"

"It's all paid up, Marie," I say with authority each time. "You're all paid up."

"Oh am I? Am I? I'm so glad, I'm so glad." And curls up, an ancient shard tucked in with a bright-colored afghan and sleeps, her mouth in a great O.

Mother and I go to the little lounge at the end of the cor-ridor. We make a stop at our usual place by the aquarium.

Nursing homes, care centers—all these final places seem to have aviaries and aquariums, where the walkers and wheelchairs are directed as if to the pleasures of a garden, the vacant eyes encouraged to gaze at another species and its floating world. Not the goldfish of golden age in the luscious pictures of Matisse and the dreamy East. This is the dark oversize fish tank of eternity, gloomy beings ghosting their way through the murk. My mother looks intently with her one good eye that isn't very good but provides her the one slice of visual reality she still has.

"Fish are calm," she pronounces slowly, with approval. All her remarks now are sibylline, occult. "Birds," she gestures over her shoulder, referring to the aviary on the first floor, "birds are flighty...skittery."

I think this is all, but no. After a long thoughtful moment, in an evenhanded tone, "Of course, they get a great deal more done. Birds."

Like Stan, she believed in work. It was what they gave to us, more than Catholicism, more than faith in the middle road—work. That's where salvation lay. And the truest love— it was in work that you found passion. *I've never had to worry about another woman. That greenhouse is his mistress.* And books were her love, at the library where she worked for minimum wage, and at home snug with a two-pounder in her corner chair, dead to the world, lost in the furies and unfairness of history, her subject. *Novels are okay, but give me a biography any day.*

Work was what mattered, what didn't let you down. Everyone has a vocation. Listen to your guardian angel—you'll know what your work is meant to be.

One night she wheeled herself out to the nursing station on third at two AM, and said, "Put me to work. I have to get a job." Beautiful Rita, working the night shift, understood. She set her up next to her at the big open desk and handed her the St. Paul telephone directory. "See if these are in order, will you, Mary?" She kept the job till the end. "I'm helping the nurses get things organized," she said. "Earn my keep."

"What's that?" she says now, pointing.

Fish in the aquarium, I tell her.

"Fish are fat," she said with some disgust. "And lazy." Great disapproval from the queen worker bee.

When I reach to hold her hand, she pulls away as if stung. "Don't *touch* me," she says, her owly eyes narrowing on me with fright or fury. "I mean it! Don't *touch* me!"

Another of her long pauses.

Then, more quietly but with her piercing Cassandra look, "Don't touch me or...or you'll lose your charm."

I find it impossible to disbelieve these remarks.

I wheel her past the fish tank to a more distant lounge. A good place that is almost always empty. There, we settle in by the big picture window. I show her the little packet of sugared lilacs. I describe the Lilac Nostalgia cake. *The Cake Bible* recommends it as a perfect Mother's Day cake. "Cake?" she asks, suddenly alert, eager.

I explain I couldn't manage the cake. I only got the crystallized lilac part done. They took the whole day, just the lilacs. She shrugs. Holds out her hand the institutionalized way she does for her pills when the nursing aide comes around with the meds cart, obedient now to routine.

She crunches one lilac down with a curious, inward look. "Pepper," she says. I feel a surge of pride: the accuracy of her still-avid palate. Still naming things, still fastening the labels of meaning, accuracy still alive in there somewhere.

We sit together by the big window, above the trees here on third. Puffy gray-and-white cloud-duvets blanket the big sky. The lilacs, I realize, don't smell anymore, once you embalm them. Sugar kills the scent. They're just the idea of lilac now, barely the look of lilac. You have to supply the rest. But here on third, that's fine. It's become obvious that the imagination is the last thing to go.

Then little Mary, all ninety pounds humped up in her wheelchair covered with her multicolored crocheted lap rug, her child feet barely touching the floor, turns from the big rolling sky, her face bright with a question she is forming.

"Tell me," she says, "do you think we'll be nearing land soon?" She lays a hand lightly on my arm, the way a stranger might inquire of the passenger reclining in the next deck chair.

It's been quite some time since I've corrected her, since I tried to reel her back— back *down* as I've come to think of this plane where the rest of us conduct our operations, our plateau of surfaces and certainty. She doesn't require an answer. I take the little blotched paw (how easily she bruises now, the skin the barest membrane, hardly protecting her from anything anymore). She turns contentedly back to the sea view. The clouds are magnificent, clearing the sky of threat.

"I like to sit," she says, not turning to face me, staying with the sea and the blue blue sky with its sketchy covering of white. "I like to sit and talk. About—about everything and nothing." She has found her meaning, what she wishes to impart to the companionable stranger in the adjoining deck chair.

We stay like this a long while. The evening moaners have started up down a far corridor. "You're a busy person," my mother tells me. "You're in your prime." One day she says, "Poor you." She's sorry she's so much trouble. "You'll do no time in Purgatory, not you," she says. "I wouldn't do all you do."

Oh yes you would, I say. I remind her that she did—her own mother lingering for years after a stroke. But I've forgotten that her mother is on the fourth floor, and though difficult, still managing.

She's right. These years I'm too busy and it's a waste. I get nothing done and I race around all the time and then I sit here doing nothing, staring with her into the bleak aquarium.

I waste my life. I want to. It's the thing to do with a life. We were wrong about work—it isn't the best thing, no matter how much you love it. Wasting time is better.

I sit with my mother, as has been destined since time began because a daughter is a daughter all her life. We stay like this, hand in hand. We have all the time in the world—*world without end, amen.* Words we recite by heart when she asks me to say the Rosary with her, the last phrase of the Gloria, the little prayer at the end that puts to rest all the Hail Marys.

Chapter 12

I WAS THINKING I'd lie down on the cot for a moment, not because I was sleepy (I knew I wasn't sleepy) but because my back ached from sitting and the awkwardness of reaching out my hand to hold hers in the raised hospital bed.

I let go of her hand and let the yellow legal pad drop to the floor between us. I stretched out on the cot for a quick moment. I wouldn't drift off—the cot was uncomfortable, and her breathing was loud. And she was dying—my mother. You don't fall asleep at this moment.

Then the nurse, the one who didn't like me anymore because of my cold-blooded obituary-writing, laid the weight of her hand on my shoulder. Someone else was in the room too, standing by the bed. She was talking to someone, the disapproving night nurse.

She's gone, she was saying.

I shot up like the risen dead from the cot, upsetting its fragile balance so that I was pitched off the side onto the floor.

"That's not possible," I say furiously as if the woman had murdered her. "I've been sitting here holding her hand." My mother's outrage in my voice. I'm on my high horse, the one she rode. The nurse says nothing. Clearly I'm holding no one's hand.

"Shall I call O'Halloran's?" she asks gently, naming the funeral parlor I listed on the form when my mother was admitted three days ago.

"No," I say. "Not till it's light."

She doesn't argue with me. I think I'm offered coffee. I say I'll sit here. "All right, then," the nurse says, that laconic Minnesota singsong. "Okay, then."

She had just stopped, given it up, sighed her last sigh, Mary Catherine Ann Teresa Eleanor. Like Dad, she waited until I wasn't there. Tiptoed out. Spare the child.

She died in the aptly named dead of night, and some primitive instinct would not allow me to leave or allow her to be taken away until the night was truly gone and it felt safe to set her adrift and to venture forth myself into the daylight. I would sit with her in this small calm room these first hours of death as I had stayed with her the last days of life.

I didn't touch her—not ever again. I sat and looked at her face. I took it in. The way my father instructed when we went for drives up north. along the river, around the city—*look, look.*

And this room, the last one, how would she describe it? *Tell what the room was like, Ma. Describe the room. Start at the beginning.* No pearliness in the gray light of the hospital walls, none of the luster she always concocted for her rooms. The walls here have the matte sheen of rolled paint. The green plants in the waiting room, the family lounge—all plastic, a fuzz of dust on the leaves. There are no flowers here. People don't send flowers to the dying. Just to the dead. The flowers will start up again tomorrow.

Somewhere down the corridor the white noise of the hospital whirs. Oddly comforting, that institutional whir. Or maybe the comfort is in writing it down, noting it. The familiar embrace of the yellow legal pad. Her kind of comfort. Words, her airy nothings.

Are you working? Are you on a deadline?

Uh-huh.

What's it about?

Oh, this and that.

The only thing to describe in the room was her little bent body turned now upward, not facing me anymore. The night nurse must have repositioned her. After. Before she woke me.

Never a bedsore on my people, she'd said, massaging the china spine earlier in the evening. *Mary, Mary, quite contrary,* she sang low and sweet at her work, unknowingly accurate as she dribbled the sponge over the old parchment of the back that had fractured once, the hip that had broken too, the airy nothings the old bones had become.

———

AND THEN THE LIGHT did come back, revealing the old wing of the hospital where she gave birth to Peter, first child. She was twenty-five, married two years. Then, beyond the dark red brick of the old hospital, the dome of the Cathedral emerged clearly, the church where Scarlett O'Hara married *the hand-somest boy*, two Depression-era sweethearts, summer of 1940, thinking there would be no war, not for them, not for America. All that was Over There. They were safe in the middle with Napoleon and Benito and mild Mr. Williams. *Button up your overcoat... You belong to me.*

And off to the side, a slice of the History Center built ten years ago atop old Miller Hospital where I, second child, her last, only daughter, was born. She liked that detail: the cornerstone of the old hospital had been set in the middle of the History Center—History not wanting to obscure history even as it razed the old building and plunged it into memory or oblivion. *You're history*—how that means you're gone, you're forgotten. The opposite of what it should mean. *You're history. Bye-bye.*

So, daylight, then. So, okay, then.

I let them take her. Called the night nurse from the room who called O'Halloran's. A man in an Eisenhower jacket came with his shining gurney in what felt like a twinkling, as if he were a little person waiting just down the hall for his cosmic cue. He wheeled her away, covered, down the white corridor, in her white gown. Shroud, I suppose it was then.

I called a taxi from the nurse's station. This felt like a solemn thing to do. Took the elevator down to the ER waiting room. I considered walking home after all. Our house is barely a block from the Cathedral and I hadn't had much fresh air in days. Or I could call home. My husband would want to come for me. Had wanted to be with me. It was I who insisted on this solo finale, had said no, go home, get some sleep.

But the taxi had already magically appeared by the ER drive.

A somber instinct kicked in. I wanted nothing personal, and no effort. No sweet husband, no solitary walk up the hill in first light. I wanted a hired carriage, I wanted to sit in state, to be conveyed from death back to life. Not to walk, not to drive, not to make any effort, not even to talk to my true love who wants to comfort me. Simply to be carried in the hired embrace of the yellow cab, suspended a while longer.

I noticed the taxi was freshly washed. This too seemed important.

The streets were empty. They felt old-fashioned, like the streets of my girlhood before the freeways. We followed the rise of Kellogg my parents would have taken on their way from Banfil and the West Seventh flats to Miller Hospital in 1946 in the driving snow. *You were born in a blizzard!* She often noted that—the drama, the witchy wink of omens, little people doing their stagecraft under the ho-hum surface of our life, sussing out significance.

The taxi glided past the History Center, then past the giant bulb of the Cathedral, turned down Summit, the avenue that so bedeviled Scott Fitzgerald. Then left onto Laurel, my street, our street, the street of my life and my love. And, as I always remember, the street where Fitzgerald, first literary hero, was born just two blocks farther up.

The taxi pulled up to our door. The driver had a soft voice, the voice of a forgiving priest in the confessional. He said the fare was $5. He apologized. It wasn't really $5, he said, it should only be $3, but the company had this $5 threshold for short trips.

"That's okay," I said. But I discovered, rooting around in my purse, that I only had a $20 bill. The driver didn't have change for a twenty. "Listen," I said, "you keep the change. Really. My mother just died. She'd want you to have a drink on her."

"I'm very sorry to hear that, ma'am," he said.

For the first time I wanted to sob—to be called ma'am. He wouldn't take the twenty. We had a little decorous argument about that. But he wouldn't take it.

"You just go in now," he said. Now he had the voice of a severe father. Not my father, but someone's. "You go in."

It seemed I had to obey him. I opened the door to the rest of my life, this new life without a living link to the old world, and he said, as if he knew all about me, "Well, now that's the end of an era for you."

Her last gift—that the first person to befriend me in the new age would be a man who understood the meaning of history.

For months, years, our conversations had been crazy, dialogue written by a committee of little people—trolls and elves conniving to give her vivid language but no sense, a cruel finish to the deft storyteller at the breakfast table with her acute eye for detail. And me, trailing along as usual, giving in to lunacy. And in the end, not unhappy about it. Wasting my life. Just gliding in the slipstream of that voice, the tatters of what was left of her spun-silk descriptions.

Your turn, she used to say, rising from the chipped kitchen table, mashing her cigarette in the toast crumbs on her plate. *Come on, you've got the gift of gab*. My turn to tell her something, a story, a funny bit from school, a sharp needle of detail plucked from the haystack of our flyover lives. But what did she want to know? What was I meant to tell her?

"You never confide in me," she would say, aggrieved. A frequent complaint. All my life she wanted me to tell her— what? "I'm praying for you," she said.

She wanted me to open my cold heart. More than that. Love was okay, but she always grasped beyond the heart. I always thought my brother fled to the West Coast to get beyond that claw. I didn't blame him. It was the soul she was after. And never any doubt that the soul existed, and that I was keeping mine from her. The sliver of self smoldering within.

"Is it about me?" she said only a few weeks ago, asking what I was working on, always pushing me to work. *I need a copy for the Archive.* It was the last time we really spoke, her hand in mine, glass of Chardonnay next to her, the two of us sitting by the big nursing-home aquarium. *Is it about me?*

Sort of, I said, not knowing what venom this might draw. Not, until this moment, hearing the avidity in the question. *And Dad. And St. Paul. The greenhouse. And you—of course you're in it.*

"Good," she said, tough as Eddie Hadro in his green visor, the crusty *Pioneer Press* night editor casting his eye over my copy on my first newspaper job. "Good. It's about time."

She dropped my hand to reach for her glass. *I like it here,* she said. *The view.*

We settled back in our deck chairs. Just sat there, side by side, taking in the bracing salt air, and faced without dismay the gauzy hinge between sea and sky, the limitless horizon dividing the elements, the disappearing point where we were headed.

Acknowledgments

To the reader, a family memoir appears to be a solo perform-ance. But its author knows otherwise. I remain happily in-debted to a chorus of family and friends whose voices have buoyed up my own. Terrence Williams, first reader, keeps me going. Stephen Williams, Rosemarie Johnstone Wein-stein, Lynn Freed, Phebe Hanson, Thomas Mallon, Edward Hirsch, and Andrea Barrett made all the difference at critical moments. Annette Kobak confirmed my faith in the memoir. Thanks as well to early editorial responses from Carol Houck Smith and our sorely missed Frederick Busch. Ann Patty, my dashing and inventive editor, gave me a new home and new hope, and who knew how much fun line-editing could be until David Hough put his laser eye to my prose? My agent, Marly Rusoff, and her indispensable partner, Mihai Rad-ulescu, have been the great champions of this book and of all I hope to accomplish as a writer. To these and to all those now lost, except to memory, who formed the world of this book, my abiding gratitude.